Notes to a Black Woman

FRANÇOISE EGA

Notes to a Black Woman

Translated from the French by
Emma Ramadan

A MARGELLOS
WORLD REPUBLIC OF LETTERS BOOK

Yale UNIVERSITY PRESS | NEW HAVEN & LONDON

The Margellos World Republic of Letters is dedicated to making literary works from around the globe available in English through translation. It brings to the English-speaking world the work of leading poets, novelists, essayists, philosophers, and playwrights from Europe, Latin America, Africa, Asia, and the Middle East to stimulate international discourse and creative exchange.

Yale University Press books may be purchased in quantity for educational, business, or promotional use. For information, please email sales.press@yale.edu (U.S. office) or sales@yaleup.co.uk (U.K. office).

Set in Source Serif type by Motto Publishing Services.
Printed in the United States of America.

Library of Congress Control Number: 2025942772
ISBN 978-0-300-27029-7 (paperback)

A catalogue record for this book is available from the British Library.

Authorized Representative in the EU: Easy Access System Europe, Mustamäe tee 50, 10621 Tallinn, Estonia, gpsr.requests@easproject.com

10 9 8 7 6 5 4 3 2 1

Notes to a Black Woman

Chapter One

May 1962

Of course, Carolina, the woes of the poor the world over are as similar as sisters. People read your work out of curiosity, but I'll never read your book; everything you've written I already know, and the truth is that it's the most indifferent people who are making a big to-do over your words. I started writing this a week ago, but my little ones run around so much that I barely have time to set down on paper the whirlwind of my thoughts. I am indignant. A girl from my home country told me such upsetting things about her life at her employers' house that I swore to get to the bottom of it. So now I earn some money and take stock of the situation: I took a job as a cleaning lady five days ago. My employers are embarrassed because I'm not fresh off the boat; I can talk about the Champs-Élysées, Touraine, or Notre-Dame de la Garde with ease. They can't call me Marie or Julie. Anyway, that's no problem for them: they don't call me anything at all.

Two weeks have gone by and no one has asked me for my name or identity card, it's unbelievable!

There are two young girls, the older one is studying advanced math, the second for her baccalaureate. The older one ignores me, she's crammed full of equations. She says: "B'jour Madame." I ask where I should put her bras, she never answers me.

The second says: "B'jour, b'soir, au r'voir," but she's won me over. In her bedroom, not a single cigarette butt; instead, in her drawer I found ten gnawed apple cores. I watch her cheerfully practicing her lessons as she chomps away at her fruit. The sight endears me to her despite her disdainful manner. There is also a delicious little boy with red hair who is quite easygoing and sweet. The two of us chat together happily.

Madame is about my age. She has barricaded herself behind a ridiculous facade of dignity and rigidity. She forgets sometimes and smiles, but corrects herself quickly. I am the maid. Madame says: "B'jour." When I arrive, I say: "Nice day, huh!"

I see the man of the house when I enter, as he leaves for his neurology clinic. He's the one who hired me. He's very tall. They all are, actually, in this family. He is level-headed and his gestures are measured; he has blue eyes filled with such kindness that I can't imagine him doing anything wrong. Madame is volatile, I think, but all women are.

May 1962

I discovered you, Carolina, on the bus. It takes me twenty-five minutes to get to Madame's house. It feels like a waste of time to do nothing on the bus. I treat myself each week to a copy of *Match;* these days, the magazine features many people of color. That's how I learned about the delicious Madame Houphouët in her evening dress. I wouldn't have written to her, she wouldn't have understood. But you, Carolina, searching for wooden planks for your shack, you're more similar to me, with your whining kids. I come home exhausted, I switch gears. My kids learn their lessons in today's fashion; they don't have much homework, that would tire them out, but they tell me in detail about the latest comic strip they were read in school. Carolina, you'll never read this, and I'll never have the time to read your words. I move quickly like all the overburdened housekeepers, I read summaries, too much is happening around me. To write anything, I have to hide my pencil or else the little ones will take it, and my notebooks too. There are nights when I find my notebooks are missing pages. As for my husband, he thinks it's ridiculous for me to waste time writing nonsense, and so he safely hides his pen. How do you manage to hold onto a pencil with your brood? Mine lose theirs all the time, and there's always mother's within reach. There is only one thing that stops them, which is when I tell them that there is only enough money for bread, and then they abstain from losing their things for a short while. They're like this with everything; it's only a matter of time before one of them brings home their shoes busted open during a soccer match. My husband says: "As long as there is bread every day, the rest will work itself out." I believe, Carolina, that you're familiar with these words. In your favela, you could never think of anything other than the daily bread. I think this is what makes me feel close to you, Carolina Maria de Jesus. My name is also Marie like you, and also Marcelle, like Pagnol—I live right by his little village, I've never read him, but I used to listen to him, riveted, on the radio—Françoise too, and also Vittalline, like no one I've ever heard of. I wonder where my parents dug up such a name.*

*The author's full name is Françoise Marcelle Marie Vittalline Ega. —Tr. (All notes are either by the translator or by the editor of the 2021 Lux Éditeur French edition.)

May 20, 1962

If I send you these pages one day, you will want to know the rest of my story. Tonight, I ask myself: "What's the point?" I am worn out. When you brought back the wooden planks for your shack, you didn't ask yourself, "What's the point?" and that gives me the courage I need to put my thoughts in black and white while my little ones sleep. I pick up my Bic again. To earn ten francs in the afternoon, I made up four bedrooms, cleaned two bathrooms and two offices, shelled two kilos of peas. For my house, I only buy them canned, I don't like to shell them, it irritates my fingertips. But I don't mind, it's the end of the month and it's Mother's Day. With my earnings I can make an enormous cake. Mother's Day—but it's really still their day! They have taken one of my notebooks again, I have to rewrite all the pages. If you had not become my muse, I would have flung everything out the window, asking myself, "What's the point of writing?" I close a window on my thoughts, another opens, and I see you, hunched over in your favela, writing on pieces of paper that you found in the trash. When I have the immense good fortune of having a notebook, a bedside lamp, and music playing softly on my transistor, it seems cowardly to drop everything because a kid ripped up the pages of my notebook. There's nothing to do but start again.

Timidly, I tell people: "I'm writing a book." They snicker. I repeated this mantra to some compatriots who saw me scribbling on the bus or in our community meetings. They laughed, they said: "Take care of your kids." Some touched their foreheads in a sign of pity. So I wrote hastily to a distant, seasoned correspondent one day when I had the desire to give it all up again. This morning, that important woman answered me: "It will be a beautiful book. I don't know what it's about, but I know the way you write." She doesn't know me, and yet she has faith in me. She is encouraging me to discover what I can stammer out, and that fills me with joy; in one go, I wrote three chapters of my *Vanished Kingdom.* The title emerged because someone had put their faith in me, with just a few words.

June 2, 1962

Carolina, yesterday was the Ascension. In my neighborhood's church, I saw a girl of my race sobbing after the communion. I was moved, I wanted to know who she was and what she was doing there, in the suburbs of Marseille in her summer dress, even though it was still fairly cold and I was wearing a large sweater. She smiled. I spoke patois, that put her at ease. She told me "someone brought me here."

"Who is 'someone'!" I cried.

"A lady who paid for my journey! I have to reimburse her 150 francs per month; I earn 220, that leaves me 70 to buy myself clothes. I have two kids back home, I worked at a snack bar, I'm not married, you know what it's like! I came so I could send money back to my mother to raise the little ones, and it'll take eight months before I can do it; I went to town twice and my 70 francs flew away. The taxi I took the first time made a long detour, it cost me 10 francs! It's all so depressing! I didn't imagine France would be like this! And the hours I work! Until ten at night! I get up at six in the morning, I don't even have time to eat!"

Carolina, my blood was boiling!

“Why don’t you do something about it? What kind of human trafficking is this! Do you have a work contract? Are you on social security?”

“No! My lady told me that she would apply for me in three months! The friend who gave my address to my boss is in the same situation; not before three months, she told me. But for her, it’s not the same, she has parents in Marseille.”

It’s true, there are many girls that are “brought” to Marseille. They leave the islands for a better future. I see them, and it’s always the same thing, they are essentially bought for a certain amount of time. Those well-to-do ladies are all the same, they want a Caribbean maid who is more nimble and more isolated than the Spanish maid before her. There are a few who draw lucky numbers in this lottery and end up with honorable and humane bosses. But there are many more who buckle under the yoke. One recounts how she is forced to clean her lady’s underwear or face punishment. Another one eats standing up. Another is brought to a mountain chalet and must go to the spring to collect water, which she finds only after chipping away the ice with a pickaxe. My husband grumbles, says I should have stayed home. “Why go fatten the ranks of this human livestock?” he asks. It’s quite simple: I’ll never be able to speak knowledgeably about it if I don’t know what it’s like.

And so here I am, I continue the ways of my ancestors, Carolina, I am of your caliber and work doesn’t scare me. For energy, on my way to work, I treat myself to a coffee. It only costs 40 centimes. To earn 40 centimes, I have to work for 12 minutes. In 12 minutes, I do mountains of dishes. How enticing that hard-earned coffee seems to me! And how miserable are those who are reduced to such tallying all of their lives. People with plenty of money don't even think about it. Those who, like you and me, know only uncertain tomorrows, but have freedom, the ability to rebel, to refuse the conditions of the slave, are the fortunate ones. How much I pity the poor girls who are told: "You can have as much coffee as you want once you're done."

When I think about their distress, I am overwhelmed with immense sadness.

June 2, 1962

It's been two months now since I became a maid, and it's not fun, Carolina. Leopards don't change their spots; to my mistress, I talk about things other than polish, Marseille soap, and clothes pins. I think she's disappointed. Her friend has "one" who speaks French very poorly and is very naive—how sweet! I seem strange to her, it makes her nervous and a little mean. She asks me:

"Have you finished the vestibule?"

"Yes, Madame."

That's the signal; she takes a dusty rug and starts to shake it out in the very place that I've just made nice and shiny! So then I have to start all over again. If I tell my husband, he'll yell, "Stay home!" and break my moped. If I stay home, I would never be able to see just how far human stupidity goes. On Monday, I clean the living room from top to bottom. I have to start by brushing a heavy rug by hand. Apparently the vacuum ruins the fibers of the precious decoration. I think it's really so she can see me bent down on the floor. On Tuesday, when everything is gleaming, Madame does her mending and hundreds of little pieces of thread embed themselves in the wool of the rug that I've just spent so much time cleaning. She says thoughtlessly: "I have to remember to put an old sheet down in front of my mending chair!" She's so forgetful! And so I go to fetch the vacuum, but she says: "I need the vacuum for the living room! Take the little brush!" *Break your back, my girl, I'm paying you two francs per hour for it.* I am a voluntary guinea pig; I suppress my desire to hang my apron on the wall and begin the brushing again. I wonder how it must be for my sisters who have nowhere to take refuge in case of revolt, who are forced to spend night and day in the company of such awful women because they have to pay back the cost of their journey! It's atrocious. Carolina, when you bend yourself over the trash, at least you have no one hovering over you to make sure you break yourself in two, and you're lucky for that, you know! When I get home, I can't lie down just yet. I have the kids to teach, to slap, to feed, and to love. Fortunately, that helps me forget about my lady.

June 5, 1962

Today, I added a few pages to my book that I had been neglecting, because last night, as my husband brought me back from town on his motorcycle, he laughed loudly: "So, your book is coming along huh? It's pretty slim! I looked this afternoon: fifty pages! You're a funny one!"

Wuthering Heights also started off slim at first. I'm so vexed that I swore to finish this damn *Vanished Kingdom,* whatever it takes. I am sure, Carolina, that no one made fun of you.

Pentecost 1962

The afternoons at my mistress's house are terrible; she is becoming more and more irritable. I was so ready for my two days of vacation! Now they're here and I'm taking full advantage. I, a girl of the wind and wide-open spaces, am forced to spin in circles in a huge apartment with closed shutters. When I enter the young girls' rooms, I'm hit with nausea; I rush to the windows and open them if the lady of the house isn't keeping watch, because she can't stand daylight. In these conditions, I long for the mistral to blow and cleanse this hermetically sealed house. I vacuum and my stomach churns, nausea washes over me from all those smells mixed together: perfume, sweat, food. But I have my revenge. I take the schoolchildren's path home. I walk the ten kilometers to my suburb, passing through flower-filled neighborhoods. I return home and I feel happy, genuinely happy, much more so than if I had stayed home all day working on some meager task of sewing or ironing. The few hours that I spend away make me appreciate my house, and I am glad to return! Even if I have to do a few extra hours of work to make up for lost time. Winter and summer, the Good Lord finds a way to enter my home. I like cleaning with large buckets of cool water, making the rooms smell of lemongrass. If I were rich, I would shun windows that gather dust and multistoried houses overlooking bustling boulevards. I would have a sun-filled house in the countryside, far from the noise of engines, and I would listen to the wind sing through the tall trees all around.

But I'm a maid, Carolina, and I twist and turn amid the stench of socks, floor polish, and air freshener, books they don't even have time to read, and young girls who never swim in the pool or go on walks.

I arrive home still feeling confined. I say to the children: "Go on, quickly, breathe," and I open up my house so that the sun enters through all the bay windows. The worst part for a maid, I think, is the smell of other people's lives. Despite my fatigue, I sit down in the sun, near a window, after I've fed the household, and I think of you. I picture you, hair wrapped in a headscarf, nailing down the floorboards of your shack, and I feel energized. The children continue to swipe my pencils, but the book progresses.

I filled out all the pages of my first notebook and I'm elated; Carolina, to know how to string words together, make sentences and be able to read them, even if what we write is pidgin or gobbledegook! It brings an incredible sense of relief. What I do comes with its difficulties: there is always a kid moaning around me and another laughing. Among them, I have two supporters: they peruse my pages, they ripped out two that seemed interesting to them, "to read in bed." My daughter found the blank pages of my new notebook perfect for drawing. I got angry, I told them that if I didn't have paper to write on, or if I was missing parts of my story, it would never become a book. Now they prowl around my blank or marked-up pages and no longer dare touch them.

There has even been some moderate progress with my husband: he laughs less, he calls me "my writer." "My writer!

Bring me my socks!" "My writer, make us a cake?" I drop my Bic pen and I make a cake. But when he leaves, early in the morning, and my supporters are still asleep, and my daughter dreams of drawing without doing so, I relish those moments: only the owl in the old pine tree disturbs the silence; I am in my element. Perhaps it is very fortunate to be able to dictate your thoughts to secretaries and have advisors to catch your mistakes, but it holds far less appeal!

June 24, 1962

It's too much! The girl from my country is in tears again. Sunday, I went to see her because she had seemed to be avoiding me for some time and I needed to find out what was going on! I climbed up the hill that leads to the villa belonging to her "masters." I found her, knee wrapped in a bandage, in a garden full of lettuce. I called to her and asked what she was doing: "Yolande! *Que faites-vous là ?*"

To remind her of her importance, I never address her with the informal *tu.* Everyone at her employers' house speaks to her casually and in slang, even the little seven-year-old girl, even the old grandmother.

"Yolande, today is Sunday, what are you doing with that spade?"

"I'm sick, I have rheumatism in my knee, they all left for the countryside."

"Who's taking care of you, then?"

"No one, I bought an ointment at the pharmacist's. The lady told me that I can't be on social security yet, and how am I supposed to pay for a doctor on 70 francs per month?"

I took the spade from Yolande's hands and asked her:

"Why are you doing this, if your knee hurts?"

"The lady said that as her maid, I have to do everything! Even the gardening!"

"Yolande, why don't you come to see us anymore?"

"The lady said that since I started going to see you I've been putting on airs, that you're the one who made me ask how she was going to heat my bedroom near the garage this winter! It wasn't you. I had to ask, it's cold even now, so imagine in winter!"

"'The lady said this,' 'The lady said that'! Well, let her say. First, you will go see a doctor, second, I will go see the lady, and then you need to wake up! You are not obliged to stay here because she paid for your journey!"

"But what am I going to do?"

"You will go to a placement agency and they will find you work. If you want to change jobs, you'll have to be registered with social security!"

Yolande is afraid of people, afraid of her own shadow, afraid of white people, like in the good old days of slavery.

Carolina, I went to see the lady, a redhead spotted with chocolate specks—like a fawn!

I said: "Madame, I am here to bring Yolande to a doctor; give me her social security declaration form."

She answered: "It's still processing! But I can call my family doctor."

"No, the doctor of her choice! She cannot live on 70 francs per month; she has two children dying of hunger back over there. How long will this continue? Labor inspections are done for her sake, you know!"

"What does this have to do with you? Who are you anyway?"

I answered: "An indignant negress. Isn't that obvious? She didn't come here to be your gardener! Where did you learn such a thing?"

These are in fact things that European women don't learn; the instinct to dominate arises in them as soon as they see a suitable target.

"Yolande gives you her entire week! She needs one hour a day to go to the placement agency."

The lady was taken aback: "But she can't leave, she owes me money."

"She's leaving, she will pay you back from the money she earns elsewhere. You didn't give her a work contract, but she can write you up a declaration of debt. How much does she still owe you?"

"I haven't counted."

Yolande dressed quickly and followed me, hobbling along; her face shone. She could finally imagine a day when her servitude would come to an end.

June 26, 1962

My mistress closes herself off more and more. Despite her dirty tricks that would have disoriented anyone but me, I remain as cheerful as on my first day; I stockpile optimism at home and I continue my experiment. Besides, I earn money for my various expenses, and a woman has plenty of little expenses! This week, I earned 50 new francs for my afternoons; they paid me on Saturday, and today, Monday, I have only two francs left. After I bring one franc's worth of lollipops back to the house, I will need to borrow from the family budget to buy my tickets. But who cares about an empty wallet when we make those around us happy and when my children are in good health? That's worth all the gold in the world! That's why I forget about Madame as soon as I am out from under her roof.

People are surprised not to see me at school when classes get out; my kids always come back alone, they claim. I have the faith of my race, I believe that they're never alone, that they never will be. On the bus that brings me to my mistress's vacuum, I invoke the Holy Spirit and He protects them. If my children get home before me, there is always a bit of damage, of course, overturned chairs, running sinks, but isn't that normal? I scold them for propriety's sake.

June 30, 1962

Carolina, they say that the future belongs to those who wake up in the morning. I have always woken up in the morning, but when the poor wake up, it's not a question of the future, but of the present. Carolina, if my feet are swollen after an afternoon of ironing, I have to massage them right away, because tomorrow I'll need to be nimble to climb the ladder: there are dozens of window panes I'll have to make gleam again. And most importantly, I need my feet to be in good shape to climb the eight floors of my apartment building: the elevator is out of service. The future, for you and for me, is a matter of the present. Madame noticed that I like the spirit and the mistral of the Holy Mother to purify the atmosphere of her alcove. She tightly closed all the shutters. In the vestibule, the thermometer shows 30 degrees Celsius, and it's the coolest room in the apartment. She turned on her fluorescent lights. I was perspiring, pushing my broom and my mop. Sweat was beading on my forehead, running into my eyelids; with a swipe of my hand, I stopped it. Thinking this gesture undignified, I chucked everything on the floor and took my handkerchief from my bag. Madame, sprawled on an armchair near a fan, said to me: "So, you think this is hot? In your country it's worse, and it's nonstop." Leaning on my broom, I told her about the immense shade cast by the mango trees, the coolness brought by the trade wind, and the windows open to welcome that wind, the shutters sucking in the air, the rivers, how we take baths in the sea. She listened to me attentively, then scowled. I told myself that the time had come to leave. But then I felt pity. The girls failed their exams. Right now, Madame is like all the mothers of the world. She felt anguish waiting for those notorious exams, pain and disappointment at seeing her children fail. Pain out of love for one's own, and disappointment out of pride: she had already spoken to her friends about the party she was going to throw if her children passed. When life has spoiled us, how can we not be prideful? I wanted to say something kind to her, but I worried about being clumsy. I looked at her withdrawn into her armchair and, withdrawn into my own thoughts, said nothing.

July 4, 1962

Yesterday, Madame left; I was alone. Two men in coveralls rang the doorbell. One was carrying a parcel in a box, the other had a tool in his hand. When they saw me, they seemed surprised. The sight of this parcel made me think of the plastic explosives that are being left everywhere right now. I said: “How can I help you?” The guy with the hammer answered: “I’m here to put up bars in the bathroom.” I was nervous, but I said anyway: “You’re at the wrong house.” The guy insisted: “This is the house, call the lady!” I was afraid of the parcel he was carrying under his arm and I said: “I am the lady of the house! If that’s a plastic explosive you’ve got under your arm, you’ve got the wrong building and the wrong people. And if you drop that parcel, I will throw it in your face.”

The things we say and do out of fear!

They burst out laughing: “You didn’t ask, but we’ll tell you anyway. We’ve already installed bars on all the floors. Last year, burglars came in through the courtyard, so we’re taking precautions. While we’re here, we came to see if you were interested! You don’t want to do the same?”

Somewhat reassured, I answered: “No, I don’t want to do the same! Now beat it!”

They headed for the elevator: “You don’t have to be so rude, you know!”

Less than five minutes later I heard Madame say rather loudly: “Who does she think she is!” She came back with the men. “Why didn’t you tell them to wait?” I answered: “What if they were here to drop a plastic bomb, with everything going on right now!” Once again, she found me too bizarre and didn’t respond.

July 8, 1962

From my home country, I received a letter from my mother along with some newspaper clippings: she told me about the Boeing that crashed in Pointe-à-Pitre. Mothers will be mothers! She doesn't want me to forget, she reports even the most minor news of the country: over the years, she has kept my heart beating, and in the cellar as I look for Madame's suitcases, since she is preparing to head off on vacation, I feel as though the trade wind has swept away the vague stench emanating from this musty den. My heart is warmed thinking of my country that has no cellars! I lug around a crate full of bottles while memories of former times scamper around in my head. And so my hours passed quickly today. Lost in thought, I forget the places and people around me, I have a universe all to myself, I am a robot, I do three times the work I usually do because it's only my arms that move while my mind is elsewhere. How many times I went back and forth between the cellar and the apartment, I couldn't tell you!

Coming out of the elevator, Monsieur's voice pulled me from my trance. He was talking to his wife: "Admit it, I chose well, it's not often you get a housekeeper like this. I don't often see her working, but she sure gets things done!"

Madame answered: "It's in their blood, those women!"

Finally, Carolina, a testimony that isn't about lazy negroes, asleep with the feather duster resting on their legs!

Chapter Two

July 17, 1962

With a guilty look, the man of the house came into the pantry before he left and placed a large bag of chocolates on top of the small broom cupboard: "That's for you, for your children. Come back in September, my wife will be pleased." Madame did not dare tell me that herself, she was so condescending to me that she's right to think I do not want to return. But what do you know: there is one member of the group who is worthy of interest. Maybe I will return after all?

August 10, 1962

For the last month, I've stopped writing and speaking to you, Carolina, because my eldest son laughed at me, he told me with his childish logic that it was ridiculous to write to a person who will never read my words. I know this, I've said as much to myself under my breath, but now he is saying it out loud, and very loudly, to the point that his brothers repeated to me in a chorus: "Yeah! Why do you tell things to Carolina? She doesn't even speak French." We don't speak the same language, it's true, but the one in our hearts is the same and it's nice to find each other somewhere, in a meeting of souls. Today, I have regained my serenity and I chat with you, I feel relaxed. As I read the book *The Imitation of Christ,* I held onto an idea: "The testimony of a good conscience is the glory of a good man." This line comes at the beginning of the sixth chapter. And yet, an easy conscience doesn't come naturally to me. Life keeps me in a state of constant revolt, not because of God, but because of man. Madame has gone water skiing with her family; before leaving, she deprived herself of food for the sake of her figure! She tried on her two-pieces in front of me, and I did see a few bulges here and there. When we are old enough to have bulges but we feel fine, why make ourselves sick trying to get rid of them? She left in a weak state, believing she had regained her figure. The girls said to me: "B'jour! B'soir!" and hopped into their Citroën ID.

I am back at home with my brood! Three months of mending await me and I have my own deep cleaning to do: that would have been enough to fill up my vacation. But no! Disaster has struck. Jean-Marc, who was playing outside, came back in with his face contorted. As he spoke, he seemed to be grimacing. I told him to speak properly; he looked distraught. I realized that he wasn't joking around, that something serious had happened. I left for the doctor with my apron still on. He told me to see a specialist immediately. I hurried into a taxi that brought me to the specialist. He made Jean-Marc whistle, lift his eyes to the ceiling, then look down, then move the muscles in his face, which gave him a ghastly grimace. The doctor diagnosed him with facial paralysis of unknown cause. I had to bring him to the emergency room of the largest hospital in Marseille.

Hospitals are marvelous. But the hierarchies we confront

there can transform them into chambers of Hell. My dear Carolina! I left with my little man, terrified at the idea that it might be permanent. The physician on duty told me: "Don't worry, it's probably a form of polio!"

At the name of that terrible illness, I felt the hair stand up on my head. And then the blood drawing began.

In an anxious voice, I asked my little man if he felt okay; he said no, and it seemed like his tight mouth had become even more deformed, his eyes even smaller.

The specialist left. A nurse told me nervously: "It's urgent! Take your son's blood and bring it with this note to the medical school, where you will ask for Madame X."

I took my kid, who to my great relief was not hospitalized, and jumped in a taxi.

The school, sad and deserted during summer vacation, seemed foreboding. I didn't know which door to use to enter the vast hall. There were many and they all looked the same. I climbed the steps four at a time. A few men in white were walking through the area. I hurried to one of them and said: "Madame X., please, it's for a blood test, it's urgent."

The other replied smugly: "Blood test? Not here, this is a school."

I insisted: "That's what's written on this paper!" And I took out the note the nurse had given me. He adjusted his glasses, scanned the note, and went to consult an orderly. "Could this be for here?" he asked.

The orderly said to me: "Maybe! Take the first staircase, it's on the fourth floor." I kept asking my son how he was feeling. He would say: "Fine, I'm okay." He was walking behind me with no apparent fatigue. The fourth-floor hall was as impressive as the ground floor. Between the closed laboratories, the empty classrooms housed nothing other than large sturdy and glossy benches that looked like immobile guards. Jean-Marc spelled out each word written on the closed doors, words ending in "gy"; in other circumstances, this place might have piqued my curiosity. But at that moment, everything seemed sinister, even the noise of our footsteps reverberating in the infinite space of the corridors. My son stopped in front of a door and read: "'Amphitheater.' It must be in here," he said, pointing. I shivered and dragged him along quickly.

I had roamed up and down the two hundred meters of the fourth-floor corridor without encountering a single soul. I returned to the men in white.

"There's no one upstairs," I said, "and it's urgent. The little one could have polio, the tests need to be done immediately. He needs to rest, too; we left home early this morning, the vial of blood in my bag is getting warm."

One of them replied: "You have to go back to the hospital and ask for more information about where you need to go!"

At that moment, Jean-Marc told me that he was tired, and his little face seemed more haggard than the minute before. I was almost yelling: "That's impossible, it's almost noon! The doctor, the people who sent me will have already left, look at the little one! I can't march him around in the sun any longer! Whatever happened to that famous human solidarity people are always talking about? Is it only for TV and the movies?"

My indignation moved one of them. He told me to wait and headed for a phone. He said a few words and signaled for me to follow him. At the end of the corridor, a young woman appeared, pretty, dark-haired, and smiling. It's nice to see a smile when for hours all we've seen is the hostile or irritated faces of people who think only of what time they get to leave work. That smile, Carolina, went straight to my heart, and the effervescence of my panicked mind started to subside. That woman in white was strikingly calm. After I explained to her what I wanted, she said in a steady voice: "You were running around for no reason! This is for me: they should have called me earlier! In two weeks, the results will be given to your doctor; give your son the vitamins while you wait. Rest assured, it will be okay!"

I thanked her and looked at my son's contorted face. I thought I had been abandoned by mankind. I made the sign of the cross and said: "God's will be done." Jean-Marc copied my gesture and my words. As we got in the taxi that would take us back to our house, I heard him murmur: "God's will be done."

My dear Carolina, after such an intense scare, saying those words made me feel rejuvenated, it was good for my Black woman's soul. A different self took the place of the one that had been in despair just before. Resignation is God's gift to the unfortunate. It keeps them from revolt, from reckless actions and words.

On the floor of the taxi was a magazine that had been left there by another customer; I flipped through it and stopped at photos of Marilyn who just died by suicide. If she'd had faith or resignation, she who had never had to lift a finger to have all the specialists of the earth at her disposal, she would not have killed herself. I felt emotional thinking about it, and I returned home with my kid and his vitamin injections, and I repeated to myself over and over: "God's will be done."

August 11, 1962

Carolina, guess what? I have an eager audience asking me for the rest of my book: my children! They read my writing! They laugh! They gasp! I need to keep myself busy while I wait for Jean-Marc's treatment to take effect, so I write. The doctor comes every other day, makes him grimace, and says encouraging things to me. To help him stay calm, I get to work; the promise of a new chapter by day's end helps him to bear his pain and gives him some joy. He approaches me and asks: "What are you writing? Read it!" I read, he asks me for the next part, and I am obliged to give him the next part, it's so relentless that my writing is starting to take shape, my husband no longer calls my manuscript slim; he even lends me his ballpoint pens, which is a big deal for him! The other members of the family correct my spelling mistakes when they can. It would be encouraging if I hadn't heard a professional writer on the radio this week talk about how it takes him three years to write a book, doing nothing but that! If I were to sit down to work on my manuscript like that, I would grow tired of the same thoughts turning around endlessly in my head. Ideas come to me one day at a time, and yesterday's thoughts change shape depending on the place or hour, I just have to set them down on paper. That said, I should have reread my work as I was peeling the vegetables.

August 20, 1962

Renélise wants to take some time off, her lady asked her to find a replacement for the ten days. So she came to see me, very amiable, very dainty with her ebony eyes and her long locks that she wears in a crown. If she wore her hair differently, she would be "sensational." Of course, she spoke to me about Fort-de-France, her parents to whom she sends a bit of money at the end of each month. "If I were at the date or anchovy factory, I would have to pay for my room and board, and this and that . . . Whereas working in a lady's house, at least this one, I manage to save some money; my lady always gives me a bit extra, I do some additional tasks for her."

I agreed to replace Renélise for ten days, she told me so many good things about her lady that I showed up full of good intentions. I learned that her husband was in treatment in Vichy and that she goes back and forth between Carry-le-Rouet and Marseille, to pass the time. She said to a young man, who was surprised to find me there that morning with a broom in my hands: "This is the woman replacing Renélise for the next ten days."

To me, she added: "This is my husband's nephew."

Madame is thin and athletic-looking: her black, bluntly cut hair gives her a serious air. She left me with my rugs and my broom and went off somewhere with her nephew. When she came back, she asked me if I thought he was nice, the nephew! I answered that I hadn't paid much attention.

August 22, 1962

This lady does not fuss over the cleaning: with her, there's no need to redo the rug ten times. I have to tell her where the most commonly used objects are—even though I have only been in the house for two days. It embarrasses me. By way of excuse, she says: "I got used to leaving everything in Renélise's care, you see," and then she spoke to me again about her husband's nephew.

August 24, 1962

I drove my children to the zoo for a bit of fun. Like every afternoon, when I leave Jean-Marc stays with his father, who has finished working by then. He would certainly have liked to go with us: the muscles of his face are back in their proper place, and the only clue that he is not completely healed is a trace of an abnormal grin. But Carolina, the others needed an escape. They bounded down the paths and for maybe the twentieth time they were mesmerized over the old lions, the grumpy polar bear, and the old animal that looks like a hippopotamus and bathes in the warm water of the pond meant for the ducks. All that excitement made them thirsty; after their walk, they mobbed the magnificent shade of the judiciously maintained plane trees. That's where the refreshment stalls are. On the benches, and just about everywhere, lovers canoodle, they think they're alone in the world. I don't look at them; it's so common in Europe for people to fondle each other wherever they go that I wouldn't have paid them any mind if my lowered eyes hadn't recognized Madame's white shoes that I had so thoroughly cleaned yesterday. It was Madame and the Monsieur's nephew, in a tender embrace. I quickly grabbed my children and moved them away, hoping she hadn't seen me.

August 25, 1962

She saw me! She asked me what I thought of Monsieur's nephew! I said: "He looks like a moron." It's not true. He looks like Johnny Hallyday! But I couldn't help myself, I pictured Monsieur sweating and panting in the steam baths (that's what she told me) while his nephew, in charge of bringing mail to the post office, was fondling his wife! When I said that he looked like a moron, Madame seemed like she was gasping for air and turned her back to me. Then, as I was leaving, she said that Renélise was a better worker than me. Tonight, I wrote to Renélise that she'll have to cut her vacation short, because I am done with her lady.

August 28, 1962

Renélise came back tonight: I told her what I had seen and how Madame had been in a bad mood for two days; she laughed and confided that she had known for a long time, and that she carried messages between the lovers when Monsieur was at home. She was the faithful, bought confidante. She even said that it was better for it to be the lady who was poisoned with her double life, that it didn't bother her. I said: "But what about her husband?"

And she answered: "He's an old pig who's always hitting on me!"

I am happy to leave that house.

September 1, 1962

I will replace someone in a bourgeois house until the fifteenth. The lady is a little shrimp, she has to lift her nose to look at me even though she's perched on incredibly high heels. She is a "pied noir" and kind.* Like her husband, she is a professor; she is exuberant and speaks in melodious streams of words! He is discreet and quiet. I've noticed that the men of the house always tend to be better than their wives, but these two seem well matched in terms of character and so much the better. They have four daughters! The girls range from one to eleven years old. Their bedrooms are like junk rooms! When I entered one, I gasped in surprise. Blue jeans hung from coat racks, dirty clothes on the floor, shoes on the nightstands. In the closets, empty tins of candy, and perfume bottles cluttering the immense library. If I'd had a chance to get "fully" involved, I would begin by giving two good slaps to those unruly little ladies and, centimeter by centimeter, I would instill order in this place. But oh well, there are too many things to do in three hours and so, stunned, I observe these Marie-Chantals.

Monsieur and Madame are away and the daughters call the shots: they come and go as they please, with their friends.

Carolina, what an experiment this is turning out to be! In a newspaper I saw an ad for a typist. I went there in person, the office manager told me that the position had been filled. She looked at me with astonishment; I understood that

*The term "pied noir" refers to those of European descent born in Algeria during French colonization.—Tr.

she was surprised by my skin color. That's how it is, unfortunately, in the provinces: you say that you can properly type up commercial or administrative correspondence, then they tell you that they want someone with experience. You say that you have experience in spades and that you pride yourself on a job well done, because of the liability of your colored skin—you know what I mean! We can't give them any opportunity to say that those Black women are all useless. We must do our work well, for the sake of all the other Black women the world over. Then they tell you to come back again, or "we'll be in touch." Then you've had enough and you go to an employment agency for cleaning women if you're in a rush to earn a living. There, the employment agent will be all smiles; the sight of a dark-skinned woman delights her: "Oh! You're looking for work? Don't leave! There is Madame So-and-So, Madame Thingamajig, Madame Whatshername, looking for someone like you."

The employment agent doesn't say: "She would like a negress," she doesn't dare. She doesn't ask for your references, if you are lucky enough to be Caribbean. The Caribbeans, because of their ancestry, are hard workers. And you will be placed with Mme Thingamajig and her Marie-Chantals and you will watch them live. The office manager told me that the full-time typist position was filled, but asked me if I knew anyone who wanted to take on a few hours with a family. "You understand," she added, "they're interested in someone like you." There was something indecent about that request, but Carolina, such is life. I said: "I'm free for a little while until school starts, I'll do it!" She found nothing unusual about it and hurried to give me the address of her friends. Just like that!

September 8, 1962

I won't say anything, because Monsieur and Madame are decent and intelligent, there is never a raised voice, never any harassment, they seem to be afraid of having such unruly daughters. Madame explained to me that over there, in Algeria, they had two "fatmas," that the girls never lifted a finger, and now . . .

September 16, 1962

Madame Shrimp is kind; I stayed a few extra hours to tidy the girls' two bedrooms; I put a label on the designated places where they must put their things: perhaps they will rip them off as soon as I'm gone, but they thanked me with a smile. I pointed out that there are no longer any slippers on the nightstands, and that it would be good for it to stay that way. I said my goodbyes to Madame Shrimp and to her family. She said she was sorry to see me go and asked me to find her "a woman like me." I understand that she wants someone who says "Yes, Monsieur," "Very good, Madame," "Absolutely, Mademoiselle." Someone who never grumbles. I don't do that because I can't stand people who grumble. But how will I find my double? There are loads of arms in Marseille, but heads that say, "Absolutely, Madame," while their spirit murmurs, "Absolutely ridiculous," I don't think so. Carolina, even if I want to be nasty with the ladies, I restrain myself, for the sake of my sisters who come by the boatful to settle in France. Oh yes, my dear, that's how it is!

Since Martine Carol brought a Créole woman back from

the West Indies to cook for her, ladies of all kinds have followed suit. They pay for the journey of the girls who want to see the country and voilà! Mulattresses, chabines, negresses, and câpresses leave the island and grab a vacuum in mid-air so that they can get to work on arrival. They are in for a surprise! I met Jeanne, she is in the same building as Madame Shrimp. A family brought her over, I met her in the elevator, a large basket of fruit in her arms. She looked at me curiously. I asked her in patois what she was doing there. She told me that she was working for a family on the mezzanine. She waited for me at the exit and told me that, in her house, the whole family was on a diet. That large girl who was used to eating a two-kilo breadfruit is now given two artichokes and an egg at night. The artichokes end up in the trash, she has never understood how someone could eat those things. At noon, she is given tournedos and four lettuce leaves. Jeanne pulled at the waistline of her skirt and said: "Look at me, how skinny I've gotten, there's nothing to eat except a bit of bread."

Carolina, this time I turned a deaf ear! I am not here to fix the mess of every girl I meet! That's what I thought, but in my head something shouted: Is this human trafficking? Is the slave trade starting all over again? My God, tell me that I'm blowing things out of proportion! My God, say to these girls who arrive by the boatful in Havre, Cannes, or Marseille, "*Quo vadis?*" Say it to them, to give my soul some peace!

Chapter Three

September 17, 1962

While I was writing my last note to you, Carolina, leaning over my washing machine (I need a quiet corner), my husband, chock full of discouragement, told me that I was writing a flop, that I shouldn't talk about things that are none of my concern. If nothing is anyone's concern, the word egoism has more meaning than ever. And he thinks that I flip through my dictionary too often, he says that novelists don't need a dictionary. Spitefully, he added: "Your book is a rotten papaya! Flowers in the wind! It will never bear fruit! You should write about snack bars, pools! Bronzed girls swimming at the beach, people like that! Who do you think will be interested in the stories of negroes?" I could have become discouraged. But, Carolina, I picture you writing by the light of a candle, without even the presence of someone to tell you what kind of papaya you are, so I bend over a new page and I fill it with reality.

September 18, 1962

The children have come back from school; they are still buzzing with the excitement of the first days: new bags and pinafores, shiny shoes, new teachers, all the happiness unique to them that we create with our sweat. My former mistress sent me a note, she has returned, her husband who gave me the big bag of chocolate added: "We would like to have you with us once more." I had sworn to stay calmly at home, but a half-day of work doesn't scare me, and also Madame didn't give me the few francs of vacation pay that she owed me when she left, so I'll go collect them.

September 25, 1962

Carolina, O Carolina! Madame was wonderful for two days and then the light autumn rain that's starting to fall aggravated her, the vacation pay she owed me also aggravated her, she paid me and her personality changed: she hid the vacuum and her brooms are worn down to the wood, and she needs the parquet floors to shine again! Now she is even more exasperating than before. She points an expert finger at the cracks, she tracks down the smallest grains of dust. She is a walking Geiger counter; she stops in front of the furnace, squints her eyes, pulls back her head to see if the buttons are polished the way she wants. She has owned the apartment for fifteen years, and there are corners that the white cleaning women have never touched. She said: "Take a chair and climb up there!" Fortunately I'm still somewhat nimble, or I would have broken my neck. The eldest daughter left for Paris, this saddens Madame and sadness makes her irritable. The one who says "B'jour" stayed. And the little boy who is so sweet doesn't talk to me anymore, they must have told him that he's too old to speak to cleaning women. When he is alone with me, he relaxes and becomes a little boy again like my own, which makes me forget his mother's disgraceful behavior. I told you sadness makes her irritable, she never gives me the time to change into work clothes anymore. I arrive at two o'clock and she's waiting for me on the doorstep.

"You will do everything, everywhere! You will get rid of all of it!"

It's crazy how much she manages to accumulate in her house in twenty-four hours!

September 29, 1962

In the courtyard, six floors below, there is a washhouse that's never used anymore. Madame saw my 68 kilos and decided to have me go back and forth between the apartment and the washhouse, with baskets of laundry in my arms! Never when her husband is there. I could have left, but if I leave, I will never know just how low a lady can go with a Black maid. It's better that I ascertain this as opposed to someone else, all the more so because I can laugh my head off with my family when I go home at night. One thing is certain, autumn is here and the water is already getting cold again. My departure is linked to the thermometer; when it is four or five degrees at the washhouse, I will know that the time has come for me to leave. After doing the dishes in the boiling water, I dunk my arms in the cold water of the washhouse for hours.

Madame thought that I'd had enough, she tried to provoke me. Thus, she thinks, the score is settled. She thinks that I am perfectly ignorant, incapable of reacting, but I think that she has trouble sleeping at night: her subconscious, at least! Eight times, I climbed the six floors because I couldn't get the elevator wet! How do you expect her to sleep, Carolina, with that heavy sin weighing on her conscience? If I tell my husband, he'll scream and I'll be forced to end my experiment. I'll just have to keep quiet and stew in my bitterness.

Since the man of the house is never there, Madame rules over everything around her with an iron fist. Her daughters never have pocket money. There is never the least bit of extra bread lying around, never extra cheese like in my home. Her baby boy has two squares of chocolate for his snack, he devours them. I know he's still hungry; when his mom isn't there, I double his ration, he somersaults with joy. There is such a difference between her and Madame Shrimp! Here, I don't have the right to drink a glass of water; a cleaning woman cannot be thirsty, cannot have any natural urges, it costs her five minutes.

October 12, 1962

Well, I feel tired, so much so that I can no longer write without great effort. I travel by moped between work and home. Once I'm driving and the mistral starts to whip my face, Madame's image fades. This year's autumn is one of the most beautiful I've ever seen. The leaves refuse to turn yellow; timidly, as though begrudgingly, here and there, one of them comes loose and falls. I drive 50 kilometers per hour. It revives me and if I weren't so cautious, I would go even faster!

Forget, forget, in the wind! Arrive back at my house free

of all resentment, with the desire to laugh and a story to tell to my children.

Faster! Faster! Drive! I forget after the fourth kilometer and the voice of reason cries out: "Slow down, you maniac! Your legs will end up in a splint at the hospital if you keep going like this." The odometer goes down from 45, to 40, finally to 35, and when I'm back home making up for lost time, only one thing reminds me of Madame: my exhausted limbs.

October 14, 1962

Madame asked me if I was going to vote: "You have to go," she said to me, "and vote yes on the referendum."* For the first time in a very long while, she spoke to me about something other than brooms and products to make the oven shine. I wanted to laugh because, my dear Carolina, I have turned to the local level to resolve my political issues for a long time now. It's my fishmonger who resolved the matter with me. She sells at the Lacroix market, she has only ever "chatted" with me in pidgin, she is old and remembers seeing the steamboats in the Old Port. She advised that I ask for my voter registration card from Monsieur Defferre and go speak my mind.† She likes everyone, she is outraged because

*In October 1962, the electorate was called upon to decide whether the president of the Republic should be elected by direct popular vote. "Yes" won by a strong majority and thus reinforced the institutional power of the then-president, Charles de Gaulle.—Ed.

†Gaston Defferre (1910–1986) was mayor of Marseille from 1953 to 1986.—Ed.

the Head of State was shot at recently, she thinks the mayor is pretty decent.*

Just as women gain the right to vote, we find ourselves in a big mess.

"Don't get discouraged," she says to me, "one day there will be as many women in the Chamber of Deputies as all those men swearing at each other. We must vote, good grief!"

I chanted: "Yes, we'll go, we'll go, we'll go."

My fishmonger slapped her hand to her forehead: "Good grief, she's going mad, the Martiniquan!" And her pity was sincere.

October 16, 1962

He came! He was here, all of Marseille was talking about it! I took the day off. I had to see what a member of the Académie Française was like! I took the bus to Saint-Loup, to the high school he was going to inaugurate. Why shouldn't I leave the brooms behind today to see Marcel Pagnol? Everyone was talking about it in Marseille, it was the day's big event. In the bus, I could feel a persistent gaze on me, I turned my head and found myself opposite a compatriot; this is fairly common and wouldn't have caught my attention

*A reference to (1) the Petit-Clamart ambush of August 22, 1962, by the Secret Armed Organization (OAS), a far-right nationalist paramilitary group that sought to maintain French Algeria through violent attacks, resulting in the deaths of nearly 2,000 people, and (2) an assassination attempt on President de Gaulle following the declaration of Algerian independence on July 3, 1962.—Ed.

if she hadn't looked extremely distressed. I approached her when the bus came to a stop and asked who she was. Carolina, you know distress, and how a sympathetic word can give us hope. I sensed that she was more unfortunate than me. I asked her if she was sick. She told me that she was from the West Indies, from Pointe-à-Pitre. She had heard that her daughter was rich, but she hadn't received a letter from her in four years. She found out her address and sold everything, her shack and her furniture. She arrived in Cannes. Between the cost of the trip, the taxi, and the hotel, she exhausted all her resources. Full of hope, she knocked on the door of Villa Saint-Giniez, which her daughter supposedly owned. She found her in a blue apron, her hair wrapped in a scarf. She thought she was seeing things! Wasn't her daughter a hairdresser in Pointe-à-Pitre? Her daughter told her right away that she was working as a cleaning woman; that was why she had stopped writing. The poor woman continued:

"I raised her on my own! I don't know why she got it in her head to leave. No hair salon hired her, besides, she doesn't have a professional certification, and yet she's been doing it for fifteen years! Now, she's a maid! I can't visit her whenever I want, her bosses don't like it. She told the sailors that she had a villa, that she was happy; of course, she had invited them over one day when her bosses weren't there, she pretended to be the lady of the house! I believed it, I came. Now, there's nothing for me to do but return. I clean! But I'm too old for this life! I have a room in La Valbarelle."

When I arrived at the high school, Monsieur Pagnol had already entered, I was told; in front of the gate, a few onlookers were still trying to catch a glimpse of what was going on.

In any event, what good would it have done me, Carolina? I was appalled by the story of my compatriot and my enthusiasm had dissipated.

October 18, 1962

Well, the die is cast; I decided to leave, because the washhouse water's temperature is cold enough to chase away even the neighborhood dogs. I gave my notice and Madame seemed more annoyed than surprised! With her personality, many people must have given her their eight days' notice. This afternoon, the ceremony of transporting the laundry basins up and down the floors began again, which "spares" the washing machine and the hot water tank; next, there were the heavy rugs to shake out on the terrace four floors above, to "spare" the vacuum. And then the stepladders miraculously disappeared in the last few days. Successfully cleaning the tiles took incredible ingenuity. Next, when she found out that a particular brand of scrubbing powder was peeling my fingers, she bought a full case of it! And then her expert fingers slid behind the radiators when I had just spent all my energy on her shelves, worse than an assembly-line job. And the handkerchiefs, direct auxiliary for sinus infections, have to be scrubbed without a small brush made for that purpose, like I do in my home! And my bile rises in disgust as I do it! And those bedrooms that smell so musty, that they forget to air out before the cleaning woman arrives. These are the details that I will never forget later, when I have the occasion to employ someone.

It all came back to me on my seventh trip to the terrace

to fetch the rugs. I hadn't planned to quit today, I knew only that the time had come, but I hadn't set a date, and then it arrived on its own; I said in one breath: "Madame, I'm leaving!" and I folded my apron. She responded: "What do you mean! Are you unwell? What's the matter with you? Give me the time to find a new person from the agency!" Now that I'm sure I'm leaving, I gave her all the time she wanted on the condition that I would no longer go to the washhouse. She accepted this compromise.

And yet, Carolina, I consider myself privileged; when I leave Madame and her dust rags, I have a home, a family waiting for me, and more work than I have arms. The distraction is immediate and the resentment doesn't eat away at me. How I pity the West Indian women who are forced to stay twenty-four hours a day with those lunatics who use them as guinea pigs! Often, they must not have the strength to eat!

October 20, 1962

I console myself about my lady's treatment, because she acts this way with everyone around her most of the time. When the children come home from school and they munch on an extra apple, the entire house trembles from Madame's hysterics. Today, it began again, the young girl devoured a yogurt without permission. Madame flew into a rage.

I can't help it! At this point, I lose nothing by speaking my opinion, so I shouted that she was lucky to have a daughter who does her equations while thinking occasionally about the yogurt in the fridge, it could be worse!

Madame is not used to anyone defying her, she listened to me in shock, turned red, furrowed her brow, and had the heart to say that I was right.

The young girl who says "B'jour!" to me all the time looked at me with curiosity and seemed surprised that I know how to speak. For the first time, she smiled at me.

October 31, 1962

This afternoon, I spent my final hours at Madame's house. Since I gave her my notice, she's become much more considerate. The man of the house waited for me and told me to stay; if it were just him, I would have stayed for an eternity, he was always cheerful and polite, tempering his wife's demeanor with kind words. Unfortunately, he leaves the house when I arrive and vice versa. Madame thinks it's a shame that I'm leaving! Who will dust behind the doors opening onto the balcony in the top left-hand corner? Not the European women! They would threaten her with legal action! Who will schlep the enormous rugs up and down the stairs without screaming bloody murder? I would have preferred that she be worse than before so I could leave happily. But what do you know, she offered me a seat while I was cleaning the shoes standing up, as I always do! And she asked about my children for the first time: she finally sees me, not as a robot, but as a human being! Well, it's too late! Perhaps I'm a bit depressed because I think, Carolina, that things could be better in the homes of Europeans who employ Black women. The little boy told me that he wants me to stay, his sweet little lit-up face moved me. I wanted to slam the door and say

“Good riddance!” but that adorable boy makes me forget the rest. And then there is Monsieur. When I declined to stay at his house, he told me that it was really too bad I was leaving, but he understood. Of course, I never told him that his wife is a pain in the neck. We don’t say such things to people of a certain status, he’s above that.

Deep down, Madame must not be so terrible, but she acted like an idiot: with people of color, they always act like idiots, as we know, but she took it too far. I can’t tell Monsieur how grueling my work was because of his wife’s volatility. I told him that I was sick, that I was tired, that my children needed me. I said goodbye, Madame stared at me for a long time, she shook my hand and I left. And so my time in that unbelievable woman’s home comes to an end.

Chapter Four

November 2, 1962

Carolina, I have a bit of a break and I'm taking the opportunity to put my "domestic affairs" in order. For example, I'm doing the medical check-ups for the kids. There are always family check-ups to do, and stores to roam to find replacements for the boys' shoes that developed holes too quickly, or their pants that they have a secret talent for ripping in the knees sooner than expected. So I schlepped two kids around with me this morning for a booster shot, and on the bus home I lost the notebook I like to write in. It happened because I was weighed down with bags and worried about a possible reaction to the shot. They both seemed fine, but that didn't stop me from asking them the whole way: "How are you feeling? Everything okay?"

I was so absorbed by my questions that I didn't notice my handbag was gone until two hours after I arrived at the house. I left for my neighborhood RATVM depot and entered the kingdom of trolley-drivers. I explained myself, and politely, after consulting a timetable, an employee asked me to come back in the afternoon. I didn't need to be told twice. At the designated hour, I showed up at the sad, gray hall where drivers were seated chatting on wooden benches.

They asked me questions. I told them how anxious I was

about losing my family's paperwork, and how I was hoping that one of their colleagues had found my handbag.

The employee at the counter reassured me: they had a bag, but what color was mine and what was in it? I listed everything and I said that most important was a notebook I really needed. He smiled and glanced at one of his colleagues. That embarrassed me, I realized that they had not only found but probably flipped through my notebook. He said that he needed the station manager's permission to return my bag, that I had to come back once again the next day.

November 6, 1962

I returned this afternoon and recovered my belongings. The guys at the counter gave me funny looks. Well, they shouldn't have read my notebook and my private thoughts.

November 8, 1962

I have a horrible sore throat that keeps me at home. Bed rest. But I don't know many housekeepers who stay in bed. Personally, I'm fine with not going out in this never-ending rain. But there are so many things to do in the house! My sons are growing up and they extend their arms to show me that their clothes are too short! I need to take advantage of my illness to sew an extra few centimeters onto their shirts.

My daughter is already becoming aware of her body. When she no longer likes a dress, she rounds her back or stands on tiptoe: "Too short! Too tight! Maman!" I pretend not to see, not to hear; I change a collar or a button color and she's satisfied.

Today, my eldest, a Cub Scout studying for his "first-aid badge," asked to take care of me. Oh Carolina, I'm telling you, it's not funny! He fixed me an herbal tea that turned redder than the autumn leaves, then he rubbed my neck so vigorously that I avenged myself by pinching his hand. Meanwhile Jean-Marc asked to be on kitchen duty: "Don't get up, I know what to do." His menu was simple: baked potatoes and trapper beefsteak, like we were camping; but with no pot, he can't make a campfire, so he'll have to wait for his father to arrive so that the beefsteaks don't become tough as old boots. I said: "You can cook the potatoes, but don't do anything else."

Standing on a chair, my chef struggled to light the camping stove and the gas whizzed beneath his nose with a sinister whistle that had me back on my feet. Well! There's a first time for everything, but even so, I guess I won't be staying in bed.

November 12, 1962

It's painful and it's persistent, this damn infection! And I am succumbing to sadness. Being sick when it's raining and cold deflates your morale. My husband, he's the motor, but I am the fuel, and when there's no more gas in the house the gears start to rust: in my home, there are five pairs of feet to put shoes on, ten sweet arms to wrap around my neck, five heads that still nestle on my chest, even though I insist that they are too big and too sensible for that. My bosom is a comfort at the end of the school day after my kids are called Chinese, negroes, pied-noirs, or gypsies, depending on the mood of the boy leading the charge. It's a merciless age and the children are nasty. I have to persuade mine that the Chinese are good people, that it wasn't bad at all to be a pied-noir, and that if negroes really were worthless, then the good Lord would not have given them souls. I said that to all of them, and they miraculously calmed down and shouted over each other, "But that's not me! It's not me!" When I'm sick, my children are lost to those young wolves, so I need to get back on my feet quickly. But my illness allows me to listen closely to the radio, and tonight I heard a woman speak. Her name is Anna, she has just been awarded a prestigious literary prize.* I stopped my scribbling, overcome with guilt. She vibrates, it's palpable, she shakes us up, and miraculously, they let her speak! Her voice is a passionate sob, and you want to say: "Take comfort in the fact that the entire earth is listening to you and wants to love you from now on." My dear Carolina, I will not buy her book, it's too expensive for me, but I am sure that Anna's pen is worthy of her voice. She speaks of extraordinary days during that vile second war, and I picture martyrs in purple robes rushed to purgatory without a passport, arriving in heaven in clothes now white as snow. Compared to all those who probably continue to die like this, those who die in our huts and our favelas, even on pallets, seem fortunate.

And then I heard the speaker talking about our priests

*Anna Langfus, awarded the Prix Goncourt for *Les bagages de sable* (Paris: Gallimard, 1962).—Ed. Translated as *The Lost Shore* (New York: Pantheon Books, 1964).—Tr.

holding councils, and I wanted to beg them to add a few lines to the Litany of the Saints: from death camps, deliver us, Lord. From racism, wherever it may come from, deliver us, Lord.

It's not that I'm afraid, but when Holocaust survivors like Anna speak out, it makes you think.

November 14, 1962

Listening! What a marvelous thing! I place a tablet at the bottom of a glass of water, I get in and out of my bed, and the voices broadcast by my old radio follow me without encumbering me. I don't have to stay put to "see," I do what I want and my imagination roams freely. I imagine each voice in the form that suits me, depending on the tone. Those voices have become so familiar to me that I dread discovering one day that they don't belong to the individual to whom I attribute them. I picture Stéphane Pizella very clearly in his evening attire, sporting a monocle, supremely distinguished. I picture Jean Nocher as a punctual school principal, smiling despite the need to project a dignified air. Georges Delamare arrives in a hurry, speaking little but well, quite old, always on his way to an urgent meeting.* These are the images I see that I'm worried will be erased by the television. Oh yes, Carolina, it's happened to me before! In front of a store window on the Canabière, I glanced at a small screen and saw a man who was speaking with a voice that for years I had attributed

*Stéphane Pizella, Jean Nocher, and Georges Delamare were three big names in French public radio in the 1960s.—Ed.

to a Tarzan. But no, I was wrong. The petite middle-aged gentleman with rheumatism who delivered his segment to the viewers was extremely likable, but I was frustrated, and for a long time I watched his sober gestures and listened to his baritone voice with a degree of astonishment. Television is the stark reality within everyone's reach; today's generation will no longer be able to dream, and, my dear, what is a life, even a blissful one, without dreams?

Ever since, I've been unsure what kind of image to assign big voices. I would like to be Madame Dussane, for the voice.* That voice says so many things, she knows what she's talking about! I don't imagine it coming out of a woman who eats only salad and crispbread. I see her doing justice to her table, portly and free-spirited! Her face? Hair maybe going gray, which she doesn't dye. It's rare that I don't like a voice, and in those cases I simply don't listen to them, no problem.

I talk about these voices because I suppose they possess a quill and, Carolina—believe me!—it makes me shrink when I think about it! Already my kid, who is only ten years old, noses around in my notebooks and tells me that I'm making spelling mistakes! So, those voices, what would they say, what would they think? My husband always gives me the right answer: "Turn off that radio and get some sleep so you can heal from your infection, throw away your notebook, you will never be a writer, that's for people who have the time to laze about! To each his own."

He's right, I know, but an infinite sadness takes over me.

*Béatrix Dussane (1888–1969) was an actress in the Comédie Française who, at the end of her career, produced radio plays devoted to the history of theater.—Ed.

I turn off the nightlight, I shut off the radio, I put down my pencil and I try to get some sleep.

November 18, 1962

My husband believes that to heal a cold, there is nothing better than to get off your butt. He came home with two tickets for the French overseas departments banquet. I complained but I went anyway: for 20 francs per person, we were given speeches, beef, and potatoes that were probably browned in lard. Fortunately the ambiance made me forget about the meal. When I saw the folklore groups arrive, I stopped counting what I could have done with the 40 francs we had spent. The Corsicans, masters of regionalist art, made us forget immediately that the banquet beef wasn't tender. The Bretons and their bagpipes made me dream of the moors, of raging waves and mists: at that moment, my husband stopped mumbling to himself that he didn't like the browned potatoes. And then the West Indians arrived! Three mulatto women who didn't know the West Indies at all! Their dancing was stiffer than broomsticks. Fortunately they had ravishing faces. I think I heard someone say that they owned a nice car. There are many West Indian women in Marseille who know how to do Madame's laundry or cook Monsieur's soup, but the West Indian bigwigs don't want those women; they know how to carry a bunch of bananas on their head, but no one wants that kind of folklore. And yet the Europeans like us the way we are, with our traditions, our customs, our lives built on laughter and tears! And then, Carolina, I almost rioted when one of those broomsticks representing my country told me that she would always refuse to sing a Creole beguine in that "language of savages." It was the cherry on top and I preferred to spend time with the Corsicans. Of course, after the group demonstrations, we danced.

I mingled with the Corsicans! It was enchanting! They told us about their dances and their songs. For the common mortal, it's banal, normal; but for me, a West Indian woman used to seeing so many classes among people of color, I observed once more that these social differences are the fundamental flaw inhibiting our progress. The people that I liked the most tonight were simply Corsican: the student, the civil servant, the fisherman, the lawyer, the guitar player, they formed a homogenous group. Never could the West Indians manage to reach such harmony, such fusion. The one who knows how to speak starts by reproaching another for not pronouncing their r's. That one who has European blood criticizes another for her skin inherited from glorious Africa. They say it in a whisper, my dear Carolina, they will never admit that they carry a bad seed in them, and yet it's true, the West Indians have a much more difficult time living alongside each other, in Europe or elsewhere, than any other immigrant community. Like a snail on a lettuce leaf, I buckle in the face of such stupidity. And our men are to blame too. When their wives wear the clothing of their ancestors, they discourage them: "What is this, you have kids and you're still wearing collier-choux around your neck and a madras on your head? Come on, it's time to put that stuff away." And the old Provençale women, like the venerable and venerated santons, wear their lace caps, which their families adore. I want to scream at those simpletons: "Men are funny creatures!" After the speeches on friendship, the bonds that unite the federated among them, they plunge their indiscreet gazes down women's blouses, size them up, and choose their first victim.

A fat gentleman spoke to me of love under the palm and banana trees. "Haven't heard of it," I said to him. He squeezed me in his arms and replied: "Impossible." He was all red; since it was a cha-cha-cha that had brought us together, I took advantage of the situation to freestyle, I escaped from his brazen chest, and I moved as I pleased, dancing for the sake of dancing, not for the guy serving as my partner. Watching me spin around him without touching me calmed him down and by the end of the song, which they played a second time, we were the best of friends.

Another very well-meaning gentleman told me how unlucky he was not to know the right "channel" to procure a West Indian maid who wanted to live abroad. He had never been able to get "one," and yet it would make his wife so happy. I answered him kindly that for this new slave trade of Black women there was an official channel, that he could simply speak to someone at city hall. He was polite, the Monsieur, he said "Really!" and asked me to teach him the beguine.

I really believe that the Frenchman, apart from being a lying politician, is not complicated. It's clear right away what he thinks, what he wants, good or bad: at least he has that going for him.

"Bunch of idiots! What's so different about your wives that they scorn the skirts of our grandmothers?" And I go on the offensive!

When I feel like it, I wear my madras on my head, I put on my floral dress with the train, and I walk down La Canebière!

People stop me, take photographs of me, ask me questions. Since Europe likes me this way, our men can deal with it!

I always want to congratulate the Senegalese, Hindu, and Dahomey women who never hesitate to wear their own attire all the time, without embarrassment, without reticence. They are many eons ahead of us, and I am learning from them.

I discussed this with my husband in the trolley that brought us home. He always tries to deflect in one way or another. Today, he spoke to me about the quality of the wines served during that notorious meal.

November 22, 1962

I am healed, and already I'm thinking of another Madame, because my experiments as a cleaning woman can't end here. For now, I am kneading the dough for my birthday cake: throughout the whole month, Sagittarius birthdays have flown like flags in the wind. The pope, de Gaulle, and Churchill all had their birthdays. I said to the children: "Yesterday John XXIII turned a year older, today it's my turn. I must, officially, be older!" Papa arrived with flowers and the boys made "paintings" in my honor. In fact, these paint smears cost me two boxes of paint tubes, but I don't dare grumble because my little girl does already, since her brothers used up her paint tubes. And then they asked my age; they forget every year. I am the age I should be, old enough to laugh, to cry sensibly. Pépé, sticking her tongue out, did the math and found me quite old. It bothers her that I'm aging: if my legs are stiff with pain, she can't dance the twist with me, or learn how to do the beguine properly. She wanted to take stock of the situation. Carolina! I wish you could have seen it! I put a record on the turntable and I reassured them all. It caused such a racket that Papa said that neither de Gaulle nor John XXIII dance, and they were Sagittariuses too! Of course they don't, but with all their worries, when a bit of joy lights up their lives, I'm sure they want to! So are they happier than me, when I can do as I please?

December 2, 1962

My infection was useful for one thing: I scribbled a good hundred pages; it's taking shape and starting to resemble a book with characters from my past; they resemble you so much, Carolina, that language alone separates them from you. The same sun shines on their sad lives, and the search for their daily bread is so similar to your own fight against starvation that I say to myself: "My God, since you allowed for that to happen, and still allow it, there must be a reason for it." Perhaps so that the rich, upon reading your journal and my letters, can make better use of what the land has to offer. Perhaps also so that we, the poor, who are no longer utterly destitute, think of those who are wading up to their necks in misery? They extend their arms, wave their hands, like you and I have seen done, and often their hands grasp only the void. So they turn toward God, their stomachs full of nothing but resignation and hope for a better tomorrow for their people growing up in the atomic age. An atomic particle! Hundreds of thousands of pieces of bread! Only the bread, with nothing on it, for hundreds of thousands of people who are starving! A little hydrogen bomb: thousands of meters of calico covering the bodies desiccated by the Pacific monsoon or the African harmattan . . . And then, shoot, I realize that I'm the one picturing this, that the reality is something else entirely. My illness is gone, Christmas approaches, I will get a newspaper to comb through the ads for domestic servants; I'm sure to find what I'm looking for. And I'll have to go see what has become of my little beggar who plays the violin when I walk by. He plays it because I give him a franc when I receive my pay from the ladies, now it's been many Saturdays since I last paid him a visit . . . He is a certified beggar, he doesn't buy wine, instead he hurries to the sandwich seller and orders a sandwich with sausage and a lot of mustard on top. For him, it's a feast. I think that's worth a half-hour of work, that stooped silhouette, that white beard, and those soft blue eyes like Jesus, awaiting my arrival. It's an answer to my prayer.

Chapter Five

December 10, 1962

Voilà: I was at the home of Madame Something of Somewhere near the prefecture. She wasn't there, but the concierge was stationed at her post, so I asked her where the lady lived.

"Why do you ask?" she replied, and I satisfied my curiosity. Poor me! The concierge told me that this noblewoman was rich but "stingy," that she didn't pay the cleaning women, even though there was plenty of cleaning to do in her home: apparently her home is like a museum!

"Don't go there, I'll find you some work." In the blink of an eye, she brought me into the milliner's on the landing, the mechanic's in the courtyard, the ironmonger's on the corner. Then a woman came, she was disabled and had a gloomy expression, she told me that the concierge was her mother and that she would help me out.

"It's better to work for people like us! When they have names like the family you were looking for, you can't imagine what a pain in the neck they are!"

I wanted to meet Madame Something of Somewhere, but I couldn't get a word in. The concierge told me that I would wash the building's six staircases three times per week. They were lying in wait for me, those staircases, as winding as the labyrinths of purgatory. Next, the mechanic came to tell me that every day I would use potash to scrub the floor of grease and the other special products used for his work. As for the milliner, more modest, she wanted me to come from five to seven in the morning to clean her workshop. The concierge was thrilled, she explained that for a long time she had wanted to get rid of a girl who was working in the building and had stolen an apron from her, sometimes drank her wine, and snatched up all the tips.

Taking advantage of a pause in her babbling, I asked: "And you're not worried I'll do the same? You don't know me."

Categorically, she said to me: "Negresses are serious workers; besides, it's not for nothing that they say 'Work like a Black'! I don't mean to offend you, but it's true!"

A boss like this would be the death of me. I promised to come back the next morning. She helpfully advised me: "There's no need to dress so well, you won't earn any tips; wear warm slippers and wool tights. It's cold in the stairwells and you'll have to wash the courtyard in front of the garage. On your way home tomorrow night, you'll take the trash cans and rinse them in the basin." I glanced at the basin, where half-frozen water was trembling. The water trickling out of the tap chanted: "Save yourself, save yourself!" I had forgotten the concierge, and listening to this chant, I smiled.

She noticed the change in my expression: "So, are you satisfied? It's a deal."

I answered:

"Still, I don't want to be rude, I would like to go see Madame Something of Somewhere, we agreed to meet on the telephone!"

"Forget it!" she retorted. "She pays 200 francs, the building shopkeepers pay 250 francs, and my daughter and I, 350 for the stairs; there's nothing to think about. See you tomorrow morning! Don't forget the trash: the broom to clean the cans is over there!"

Crystalline, the water sang again: "Save yourself, save yourself, quick." My dear Carolina, I didn't need to be told twice: practically running, I took my bus home. What would have become of me working for that concierge? Laughing, I recounted my adventure to my family. My husband was in a closet grabbing me a pile of mending that I was planning to do overnight. He didn't laugh, he was almost angry: "One of these days, you're going to end up in a nasty situation! You have work and bread at home! I've had enough of your ladies!"

Bah! Once he's calmed down, I'll go back to the employment agency and ask for the address of another lady without a concierge.

December 24, 1962

It's so cold that, even if I had a lady, I wouldn't have gone to work: the moped is in the cellar and patches of black ice adorn the city sidewalks. Marseille, stunned, shivers, doesn't understand. I've caught up on my mending and my book has been enriched by a few new pages. It's funny, a first book is like a first child. The hands and feet of the inert embryo grow: we wonder what it will be like, this little baby who wreaks havoc and makes us nauseous; we can only imagine it will be beautiful. I won't say that my scribbling is a masterpiece, but I like to think that my book really is alive: when the children happen to read a few lines of it, they ask: "And then what?" I believe there is no better judge than them; since they want to know what comes next, it is worth the effort to write.

December 28, 1962

Each winter, depression takes over me, invades me, and dissipates only in spring. With summer still six months away, I must continue to live. I went by the place where "my beggar" usually is; the sandwich seller told me that an ambulance had picked up him along with his violin: he had passed out in the street and was in the way. That disturbed me: I loved to listen to the songs he played on the strings of his violin; he hummed along to "O Magali" with an authentic Provençal accent. I am really disturbed, Carolina.

It's gifting season, and I hate receiving gifts without giving: a lady who pays three francs per hour would do the trick, but it's too cold and the basins on terraces or in courtyards would kill me. My harsh experiences in others' homes make me appreciate my own and cover my extra expenses.

January 3, 1963

The girl that I plucked from my neighborhood wrote to me. She has climbed the ladder of society, she has "risen" to Paris, she is a cleaning lady in a hospital, it's not ideal, but offers a taste of future freedom. Carolina, this is what she said to me—it's simpler to rewrite her letter than to explain it in my own words:

"Only West Indian women do this work. It's not fun, but I

see my compatriots and it gives me strength. They say that I could become a nurse's aide after this. I've been in Paris five months and still haven't seen much: I always take the metro, it's faster; I have two days off per week, I use that time to write to my family, do my laundry and a bit of cooking. I live by Quai de la Rapée, the Seine is the only thing opposite my window. It transports ice cubes at the moment, and fog keeps me from observing the barges there: it lasts nearly all morning (the times when I'm here). I share my room with two other West Indian women, they also work in hospitals, sleeping isn't an issue because one of us is always working a night shift. It keeps us from being too cramped. The landlord gives us a receipt in one of our names for 7,000 francs, and individually we pay 20,000 old francs: my two roommates have a proof of residence document. I've never gotten a receipt for the 20,000 francs I pay, I can't do anything or say anything, it's like this everywhere, and if I do, I risk being kicked out: in this cold, that's no joke. Things are tough, but much better than in that lady's home in Marseille.

"Thank you, . . ."

Carolina, this is the Parisian idyll of West Indian women, and they continue to flock there by the boatful, some to live on family allowances just like the French, others in hopes of making more substantial money, and the metro engulfs them, the factories gobble them up. So they become shells of themselves; they don't laugh anymore like they did in Fort-de-France or Pointe-à-Pitre, they don't have the time. Sometimes they find peace in a sanitarium, or a lot of money near Clichy, and voilà, they traded the hut or the favela for the hovel and the hope that never leaves the unfortunate.

My compatriot's boundless happiness perplexes me: I

won't discourage her, but I am as concerned for her as for my beggar who was picked up off the sidewalk.

January 6, 1963

Cécile arrived in the "West Indies" of France: she traversed the country from Le Havre to Marseille searching for sun. The sun is there, and always will be, but it is frozen by the wind that blows over Mount Ventoux before rushing through Marseille; the cold penetrates the thickest coats and everyone seems to have an invisible pipe, smoke blows out of our nostrils and our mouths. This natural steam frightens Cécile, she came to tell me.

Each time, I swear I'll mind my own business: why did she need to come to Europe when the temperature drops to negative eight here and the wild boars are a stone's throw away in Provence? They emerge from the forests looking for food and instead meet their deaths. All the butcher shops in town serve them up, and even sell squirrels by the half-dozen. They're easy to hunt in this season. Did Cécile not know this? Someone gave her my address, someone is always giving out my address to West Indian women having problems. I'm not happy about it. Carolina, each time I decide to be horribly selfish, God punishes me and sends me some food for thought. Well, when I saw Cécile this morning, her long fingers horribly swollen, all I could do was tell her to come in and wait for her torment to subside. She was a certified accountant in Fort-de-France, she even had a maid. She made the rounds of the employment agencies in town, she was sent from one job to another: they took one look at her dark Black skin and said politely, "I'll be in touch." The first week of December, she waited, she didn't know what "I'll be in touch" really means in France, and then she must have accepted her fate, because she needed to pay for her little room in Le Panier.

She took a job ironing in a sordid laundry in her neighborhood. She lived in the steam spewed by her iron that sprayed water of its own free will. And then she agreed, to earn some more money, to wash a baby's clothes when she gets home at night to her room with no heat. The result was not long in coming: chilblains all over her hands and feet. As she talks to me, she rubs her feet together to relieve her itching. She looks at her fingers, ready to burst, and a tear pearls on her long lashes. I can't start crying with her, what good would that do? I put on my hard shell and said: "This is how it is in France, what did you expect? Not everyone has a manicure like the Baker girl,* and to earn your bread you'll have to work and take care of your hands and feet. First things first, put your suitcase in my daughter's bedroom. Get out of Le Panier, or you'll die of depression before the end of winter. Warm yourself up, I'll go to the neighborhood biscuit factory to get you a handler job, that will tide you over until your fiancé returns from Laos. On that note, why did he have you come so early, since he still has six months left over there?"

Cécile understood from my gruff tone that this was an order. I absolutely had to fix her gears, which had been

*Josephine Baker (1906–1975) was a famous Black singer, dancer, actress, and member of the Resistance. She was born in the United States and moved to France in 1925.—Ed.

jammed by winter. As I write to you, she comes and goes, and I even saw a smile light up her ebony skin. Carolina, do you find me ridiculous? By this time next year, she will only be a memory, but the present moment is enough. It's cold, a girl from my country is warming her body and heart under my roof, come what may.

January 12, 1963

Cécile is a warehouse handler and fine with it: she will have plenty of time to be an accountant again when she returns to her country. She says that she's happy, I won't contradict her. And the cold continues. The concierge wrote to me: she kept my address, despite my voluntary "retirement." She found me work! Again! I am wary of winter and of her. I watch my book take shape, Carolina, and I rub my hands together. The afternoons are long and calm, only winter calms the Provençals, it allows me to write, another two chapters and it will be finished! But when it's finished, what will I do with it? It's time to start thinking about it! I'll ask the advice of a French woman who knows how to read well, write well, and who is not merely a "Madame à trois francs de l'heure."

January 20, 1963

How can I not laugh when Solange comes to visit? She arrives with her truckload of humor, she has the gift of seeing life through rose-colored glasses. Solange is my daughter's godmother. She's a prickly mulatto woman who refuses to speak French, even to "her ladies." She finds an intermediary language between Creole and Voltaire's tongue, enough to be understood. She claims that when she doesn't mix a few syllables of patois into her conversation, she feels the cold much more.

"I know that you stay home when it's cold; I came to say happy new year before the end of January. I'm not working, I gave my notice to 'my lady.' Can you believe it, I caught her standing on a chair turning back the clock in her vestibule! The half-days had felt so long recently! I cursed the buses that always brought me home so late. I even gave my wristwatch to a watchmaker to be repaired—nothing worked! I always arrived a half-hour late. And then, on Christmas Eve, I needed to buy some mistletoe for my nativity scene, I went to tell 'the lady' that I wanted to leave a bit early, I saw her, yes, my dear, *saw* her pushing the large hand of the clock with her finger, a half-hour backwards! I thought I was dreaming and I vowed to keep an eye on her; the entire week of New Year's, I saw her doing the same thing. So, the day before New Year's, I told her that she owed me 120 half-hours, that she could come down from that chair. Her family had traveled in from all over. She barked at me, asking what was wrong with me, if I was crazy, and I told her that I had been watching her for eight days and that for the last three months, without understanding why, I was always getting home late. That monster turned red with embarrassment and I turned red with anger; I threatened to bring legal action against her, she paid me what she owed and called it a Christmas gift, she said that she wasn't admitting to my accusations. And so I gave her my eight days' notice, and I stayed home! Stealing a half-hour from a poor negress, when they're about to fly off on a ski holiday! It's degrading, don't you think?"

And Solange started to laugh like only she can.

Then Cécile arrived with a tin of cookies.

Solange asked: "Who is this negress? A new one?"

I introduced them. Solange observed Cécile's gentle face and her steady movements. She tore at her hair and cried: "Someone like you should never work in a lady's house. What are you thinking! Twenty years I've been working in others' homes, or just about. I arrived at the end of the last war, when people were eating rutabagas and saccharin. I stayed for six years with one woman, I raised her little one like my own daughter. She spent more time with me than with her parents, and then one day I went to fetch her at the end of school, and she stopped holding my hand as she had done for so long: she had just realized that I was a negress, she told me to walk behind her. Her parents must have said something to her. I stayed a few steps behind her, and it hurt me so much that I packed my things and left. Since then I work with my hands, not my heart. As soon as things go south, I don't try to understand, I go elsewhere. From time to time, I check the rates at the employment agency, that's all. I was a hairdresser back in my country, I defrizzed women's hair. Here, the women want to have their hair frizzed. Despite my references, I couldn't get a job, and I had to eat. I was never able to get out of that cycle: once you're reported to social security as a domestic servant, go ahead and try to do something else! My husband is a sailor, his home base is Le Havre. I can't stand the fog, so I stay here. He comes once per year for his vacation, I have no kids!" She stopped messing around. "The little girl I raised would be nineteen years old now. I liked that little girl a lot, with her blond curls. I styled her hair in ringlets! And now . . . I've become like this . . . indifferent! So don't go work for ladies with your donkey eyes."

Like a gust of wind, Solange was off again . . .

She laughs, but she's in pain . . . She suffered a shock, Carolina, and nothing can heal her. I laugh with her, so as not to rub salt in the wound.

January 23, 1963

Cécile's parents wrote. They want me to tell her to go back to the country if her fiancé is taking too long to return to France. Meanwhile, from Laos, he thanks me and asks me to keep his future wife under my roof until May. Cécile tends to her chilblains and settles into the factory. The forewoman addresses her informally, her new colleagues do too, but they like her, she has a very well-meaning friend who made her a schedule for the coming year: until Easter, they'll stay at the biscuit factory; in May, they'll move to the canning factory to put anchovies in tins. During summer vacation, they'll move to the lemonade factory and then to the date factory. Meanwhile, they'll go to the ball in winter, and swim in the Calanques in summer. Her friend has also solved their man problem: they'll spend time with a new one each season until they pick a winner. Cécile is a bit frightened, not out of hypocrisy, but because she wonders how her friend can slobber all over her current lover in public when he comes to meet her in front of the biscuit factory. "And just think, back in my country, I couldn't even walk arm in arm with my fiancé through my neighborhood." Carolina, what do you want me to say? "Do your training and keep quiet!" It always ends on a cheerful note. Cécile asked me what I write in the early morning, when the kids are asleep. I felt caught in a trap: I said I was doing some work for a printing press. It's a good excuse; I write loads of addresses on strips of paper for a publishing house, they pay by the hundred. You'd have to do a lot to earn 500 francs! What would she think if I told her that I was writing a book and that I'm on the final chapters? I still need my anonymity; without it, I would lose my confidence. And yet, if I want to know what my baby looks like, I will have to extricate it from my house so that people can tell me how it is. Cécile reads many good books; she has sound judgment and understands what she learns. Maybe I should try talking to her about it one of these days?

Chapter Six

January 30, 1963

The unfortunate who are ignorant of their plight are the happiest of all. I went to my friend Roland's house with my husband for his daughter's baptism. It was very cold, and we had to push our motorcycle the whole way: the patches of black ice kept us from driving. This exercise lasted three-quarters of an hour before we arrived at our friend's house in the middle of town: he's proud of that location, but I don't envy him. It wasn't until adulthood that my legs encountered the winding staircases of big cities, and it always repulsed me to climb up all those floors. We grabbed the small parcel for the baby from the motorcycle bag, and we waited awhile in the hallway for our feet to thaw; then we tackled the hike up the building to where Roland and his family live on the top floor. Janine, beautiful as a fairy, opened the door for us, and Roland, happy as a king, introduced us to his daughter. They are quite different but suit each other well: Roland is a Martiniquan strong as a Turk who works on the docks, and Janine is a blonde from Vaucluse who seems head over heels for her husband.

We entered: the pane of the transom window is broken, so Janine placed a piece of floral fabric over it to mask the hole, but that doesn't stop the mistral from entering the room. She lit her gas stove to heat up the hovel. My dear Carolina, this hovel may be in the middle of Marseille, but it's like any favela: a single nuance differentiates one from the other—whether the people living in them are optimistic or hopeless. This couple is optimistic: nothing discourages them, not judgment, not their hovel, not the precarious life they lead.

The guests fill the two rooms, a half-dozen of our compatriots all accompanied by Europeans. Roland boasts that he chose the most beautiful one, and he's right. Janine has three children, but she's managed to stay as fresh as a spring day, her long copper-colored hair tumbles over her pretty face. She is all smiles, and her eyes glittering with gold outshine her surroundings. Roland loves to see her looking radiant; he gave her a black tulle dress decorated with silver dots. He said: "I bought it on rue Saint-Ferréol, since I can't buy her an apartment. At least her family won't be able to say that I don't dress her!"

The baby's godmother is a Spanish woman clinging jealously to her husband, who looks like a gorilla. There is also Janine's neighbor, wearing a garnet-colored velvet dress that flatters her figure. She is there with her four children, making sandwiches. And then another doll, platinum blonde, who doesn't even glance at us, so busy is she being wooed by a little Guadeloupean man with mischievous eyes. All those women in their cocktail dresses shiver in this hovel, but insist on showing off their bare shoulders. I am a sorry sight next to them, with my wool pants and baggy sweater—I even kept on my boots.

A heap of victuals sits atop the old sideboard, which has been painted white. The women smoke to appear chic, and we are enveloped in a grayish mist. Janine is kind and I like her a lot. I take the baby from her crib, and immediately, in the corner where I've retreated to, the children surround me. From there, I can calmly observe this strange universe. I said to fat Francis that my shoes prevented me from dancing the beguine, so the other men left me in peace. I prefer the company of children. The other women say nothing of substance: one thing is certain, they find me trustworthy and confide in me. Janine wishes her husband's sisters were more like me. Well, Roland has chosen her: I'm always telling him to stop flirting with other women, since he already has three children. Janine appreciates this and wants me to encourage Roland to legalize their relationship, since for now they have a common-law marriage. I've already had one victory: they agreed to baptize the newborn, whereas the others were not baptized. Their parents were too busy throwing fits of jealousy.

I met Roland one night when he came with my husband to reimmerse himself in the atmosphere of a West Indian family. He said that he was sick of his in-laws, who called him a filthy Black. I told him that he wasn't in a relationship with his in-laws and that he should focus on his children and his wife, who loved him deeply. I think that cheered him up, because the next week he brought Janine over to meet us. That's when I learned that they weren't officially sanctioned in the eyes of men or God. Roland believed that baptizing children was a woman's affair, and his wife wasn't religious. As for marrying . . . He would rather do it in the West Indies, far from his in-laws, and so he keeps indefinitely postponing the event.

Nevertheless, I was able to convince both of them to baptize their forthcoming child by appealing to Roland's pride. I said: "You've become a pagan, but your mother didn't raise you pagan! I'm sure that as she carried you on her side while toting her baskets of fruits and vegetables between Tivoli and Fort-de-France, all she could think about was your baptism outfit! For her, it was a sacred tradition. Why are you trampling on all our customs now that you're in Europe?"

Janine caressed her rounded stomach as she listened to me: "Hey, Mamèga, the baby kicked while you were speaking. It will be baptized. We don't really do that here! At least, it doesn't have the same importance that you West Indians attach to it!"

I started to think of the happy times when legions of missionaries came from neighboring continents to evangelize the hovels, the housing projects, the villas, all of Europe. Janine shook her long copper hair and laughed, laughed, it seemed unthinkable to her. Imperturbable, I continued: "The Indians believed in the sun or a totem, Black people in their talismans, the Asians in their dragons, in their sun, what do I know! But at least they believed in something, good or bad. The landscape has shifted. The older European generation no longer believes in anything, it's all a formality! The few who escaped from the mêlée go elsewhere to tell those with a spiritual ideal that it's not real and they forget their own flock, which has gotten completely lost!"

In the end, the little mixed-race girl was baptized and it's all thanks to me, Carolina! I hold her in my arms, she is ravishing, and I forget that I will have to face the black ice to get home. Roland plugged the record player into the ceiling, he installed a power strip under the bare bulb that casts its crude light over the guests: you have to duck down to pass under it so as not to rip out everything. And then those damn West Indians got tired of the music on the records! Roland drums his hands on the edge of the table, another hits two forks against a bottle, and the guy who was wooing the platinum blonde taps his heels to the beat. This improvised jazz fills the garret; the radiant Janine and her eldest daughter, their hair swaying from right to left, intoxicated by the rhythm, get into the groove. Janine's neighbor, a widow, lets a large beanpole of a man squeeze her tightly. Her little six-year-old boy who hasn't left my side for one minute since I took the baby in my arms asks me why the man is staring at his mom, and his sister, nearly a young woman, blushes with embarrassment. I pick up on her discomfort and I have immense pity for that girl who had no need for this spectacle. I talked to her about the snow that refused to melt in my neighborhood: would she come visit me one day? She seemed to forget that a large Black man was kissing her mom who was swooning with pleasure, but I could tell that she was preoccupied despite my prattling. My husband joins the orchestra; I'm pleased. But that platinum blonde better not dance with him. For another hour, they danced, they spoke patois: if the mistral hadn't pierced through the curtain covering the transom windows, it would have felt like a picnic in the West Indies.

Before we left, Roland, so bull-headed, said to us: "I will marry that woman this year! You will be our witnesses." I said phew! Janine doesn't know yet about his resolution, but I am very happy for the three children.

Back at home, I told Cécile what had happened and grabbed my notebooks to add a few words to the end of my book's final chapter. Cécile was bold enough to ask me what

I was writing in the notebooks piled up on the table. Suddenly I declared: "I'm writing a book!" I expected mockery; she didn't laugh and I was surprised. So, emboldened, I said to her: "Read one of them if you'd like." She nestled into the corner seat and devoured one, two, three, four notebooks. She interrupted her reading to say: "Hey, this is really good! It's so true to life! You'll certainly be published."

For the first time, I hear this word and feel a bit frightened.

February 2, 1963

For nothing in the world would I miss going to the Abbey of Saint-Victor for Candlemas. I set out today, despite the cold, hoping that it wouldn't be too crowded. No such luck! Carolina, all of Provence, or rather all of the Marseille region, had come to kneel down before the Black Madonna in that Byzantine church. The navette sellers had lots of business, swamped by a flood of buyers, their temporary stalls set up right in front of the abbey's now too-narrow entrance.

I had never known whether that statue was made of stone or wood, such a highly revered object whose origin has been lost to the mists of time. She carries a curly-haired Baby Jesus high up in her left arm. She is dressed in sumptuous green fabric. I confide in her as I do in you, Carolina: with her dark complexion she is so similar to me! Normally when I pray the Hail Mary, I know that this is the queen I invoke, but I ask forgiveness for appealing to her, in case she wasn't made for me. Here, it's different: during the fleeting moment when I approach the statue, after waiting in a long line of people, I find that she has the serene expression of women from my country who have struggled throughout their entire existence; perhaps I see my mother's smile, the demeanor of women whose stories soothed my childhood. I am infinitely grateful for this illusion and egotistically I believe she was made for me. I follow the line, I descend once more into the abbey's crypts designed by the famous architect Cassian; he did his job well and those old stones will last for centuries to come. I glance at the tombs of the martyrs, sometimes unknown, who rest here, and I envy all those peoples who have only to look to find the history of their past. I cry out in the depths of my soul: "Where is my past? Is it a void?" Then the Black Madonna's smile reassures me, calms me. Isn't it true, Carolina, that we must be stupid to think such things?

Armed with a few altar candles that I touched to the Virgin's jewels, I feel strong enough to face life head-on. For life is not only thoughts, it is reality, and my reality is a difficult thing on this February 2: I spent the last franc of what I had saved up over the three harsh months of winter. I will have to find a lady not for my experiment, but to deal with pressing matters, or else I'll have to turn to the pawnshop soon. The grocer on the corner puffed out his chest and announced to his stunned clientele that parsley was taxed at 12 francs per kilo: from now on I'll have to pay that. The price of potatoes is astronomical. Those in the neighborhood with liver problems no longer eat the artichokes; they buy them and use the juice to heal their liver, at three francs per kilo. Spinach has become a luxury item and lettuce is taxed at six francs per kilo. As a result, all the domestic servants buckle under the weight of the family budget, and the most determined have already found a job.

February 6, 1963

Cécile's fiancé arrives at the end of April; she is ecstatic. With a feverish hand, she caresses her white wedding dress that an expert seamstress fashioned for her. I had never seen the dress, she didn't dare show it before her wedding date was set. It will take place in early May with the blooming of the daisies, lilacs, and peach blossoms. It will certainly be more cheerful than in winter.

February 8, 1963

I heard on the radio this morning that two West Indians killed each other. I listened closely but I didn't manage to catch their names. My husband came home at noon; he seemed distraught, he squashed the tear forming in his eye and said: "Roland was shot right in the heart on a street in Harlem." Overcome with emotion, I dropped the plates I was holding. It made a racket that gathered the children around me. When they heard the news, they all started wailing. They knew Roland well, he would come to our house on his big motorcycle to entertain the children. He would put one in front of him on the seat and another would hang onto his jacket behind. My boys were always thrilled. And Roland would sit with them under the pine trees and tell them a thousand and one stories: his battles in the Jonc Plain in Indochina, his co-workers who would carry tons of bananas each day from the boat-holds to the docks, the crates big as armoires that they would carry single-handedly. He would flex the muscles of his Herculean arms and the boys would try to imitate him, in vain: it always ended in bursts of laughter. Spending time with them rejuvenated him, and he would set off again to lead his life in the fast lane, between the docks, his garret, and Harlem.

We went to the mortuary of Cimitière Saint-Pierre to find out the time of his burial. The caretaker told us that we could see the Martiniquan, they had done his autopsy and placed the body in the "refrigerator." Roland, in the refrigerator like some kind of chicken! When just eight days earlier he had brought Fort-de-France together in his hovel, had decided to get married, to settle down! It was unthinkable. I had no choice but to believe it when the caretaker slid open the compartment and showed us Roland, asleep forevermore. I tried in vain to close his half-open eyes. He seemed to be smiling, to be telling a final joke to those who knew him. I said my De Profundis in front of the indifferent attendant.

In the afternoon, we returned for the burial. Blonde Janine arrived in hysterics, her long sun-colored hair mussed by the mistral, dressed in a black leather coat. The little widow who loved to flirt gave Janine her arm and the Spanish woman accompanied by her gorilla husband walked behind them. One by one, Roland's friends arrived. I had never met that group, dockworkers with their eyes concealed by caps, day laborers, and a band of idlers who had taken advantage of the bus that drove the procession and who, out of curiosity, had come to feast on the grief of others.

They spoke, they laughed in front of the open casket, their chicks had come with them, who were more decent, although made up and in short skirts. Finally, a petite woman dressed in a mink coat came out of a long car with an enormous wreath. She disappeared behind the flowers so that her cauliflower hairdo was all you could see. A murmur went through the motley crowd: I realized that this was the mistress who I had thought was just a figment of Janine's imagination. All eyes were on that woman, and the onlookers had a good laugh. It was revolting; I let go of my husband's arm and spun around to look at my Black brothers and said to them in patois: "So, there's no saving any of you! You have no respect even for a dead man, and not just any dead man! Your friend had no relatives here, you were all he cared about, all he talked about, to the detriment of his family, how to help you get another day of work on the docks, how to lend you a few francs, to find you shelter when you arrived illegally in Harlem. Today, you laugh. You're all disgusting."

My dear Carolina, these are guys you don't talk back to, they're quick to use their fists and even their blades, but one of them said: "Hey! This woman talks like my mother! Just like her! She knows how to put people in their place. Men, enough!" They went quiet, they stopped laughing. I was happy to have restored them to a semblance of dignity for a few moments.

But Janine broke the spell, she bounded like a tigress when she saw the blonde woman and the giant wreath, she yelled: "Get that wh . . . out of here! Roland got into trouble in Harlem on his way to her place, she's the reason he's dead!"

The mortuary attendant had seen it all before, he said: "Family over here, please! It's time to lower the casket!"

In three seconds Roland disappeared from our eyes; Janine was crawling on the ground. The funeral director had taken the wreath from the woman in mink, her mascara was running and her eyes were red with tears; she hadn't said a word. Faced with her silence, Janine calmed down.

Amidst all his favorite hooligans, Roland was lowered into the ground. There are no words to describe the thud of European dirt closing itself back up over a man who constantly spoke of returning to his homeland on a giant boat with his family, of shacks on the hills of Tivoli, of the sun on the Chapelle du Calvaire in Fort-de-France. Roland lived here, but he never adapted, he was still searching for his sky among these thugs. There's no name for this, it's better to forget about it.

Janine tried to throw herself into the hole, but the hooligans said: "What a load of crap, it won't last, she likes men too much, you'll see!" I fled because there are moments of sincerity that must not be tarnished by doubt.

February 16, 1963

We've stopped talking about Roland around the clock and I can finally collect my thoughts. I was able to send a few pages from my book to an important woman who likes the West Indies and West Indians, my dear Carolina. She wrote back to me quickly: "I devoured your excerpt, I was immersed in a bouquet of perfume and poetry. You must keep going with this book: one hundred times yes, it's so beautiful . . . " Well, I could have jumped for joy, now that I have an audience of two people, not including my family who are awaiting more of my writing. But I'm not jumping for joy, because I'm so anxious about what will become of all my hours of setting words on paper. Cécile told me that I should stop working in ladies' houses, that I should write books, many books, that it's worth the effort. I had to laugh. To publish my work—me! I don't know anyone involved in such things,

I don't have a penny left, and it's already fall. I can't even rely on a sensational physique that would attract someone's attention, so how will I get my foot in the door? Cécile is twenty-two, but she knows the right words to convince me. She says: "Mamega, believe me, this is good! If I could write, I would do it. You can't give up." A supporter like her, who repeats the same words to me every day, keeps me from throwing in the towel; for when my wallet is empty, I trust in nothing but the bank notes that will allow me to do my shopping today: it's only the fifteenth of the month and my husband's pay has flown away. How can anyone be a lamplighter or a mailman and have a bunch of kids! And the winter is never-ending! The snow has come back to frolic through the south of France. Utterly unfaithful, the snow has abandoned her Nordic home this year to rollick with the mistral. And the wind pitches and makes the pine trees weep. The surrounding areas don't have last month's thick ermine coat, the white covering is thin and fragile; fortunately the sun joins in and pokes holes in this unprecedented cloak.

February 18, 1963

I saw a classified ad posted on the scale at the bakery: someone is soliciting a cleaning woman two days per week. I asked for more information and learned that an old woman living alone, not far from my house, is looking for an aide. The long, long winter has trapped her inside her little apartment. Carolina, I didn't go for the sake of loving one's neighbor; I wanted to earn 600 francs in two hours, and it was nearby! But there you have it. I was shaking out everything in that shack with its piles of dust, I scrubbed the parquet floor and scoured two full tubs of pots and pans while the little old lady told me about her misfortunes; her children no longer look after her, she lives on nothing but her old-age pension. I listened to her, I worked hard; the grandma doesn't have a washing machine, and I had to deal with a half-dozen sheets. Two hours weren't enough to put the place back in order. The little old lady anxiously consulted the old clock:

"It's time!" she cried. "Two hours is enough!"

"You've got to be kidding, two hours! This place needs days, grandma! You've neglected the apartment for three months."

She counted and recounted the coins for me and asked herself what kind of "stubborn mule" had invaded her home.

So she spoke to me in pidgin to explain that she only had 600 francs. I said: "All right grandma, I'm finished: keep the 600 francs for a nice pot-au-feu! I'll pay you a visit sometime!"

She couldn't believe it, and was so afraid that I wouldn't come back again that she cried:

"I can give you 600 francs for a month, two times per week: by the end of March, I'll be back on my feet and I hope social services will send me to a nursing home."

"It's okay! You aren't satisfied with having a cleaning lady for free for a month? It's pretty unusual, and I typically charge a lot, you know! When the ladies see my 72 kilos, they hire me on the spot, and I take their money without hesitating. They're not mean, but they're imbeciles. But you, grandma, I wouldn't eat what I bought with your money. And to think that your children are ladies strutting about somewhere without a care for you!"

That's why, Carolina, I have a lot on my plate for the next month.

Chapter Seven

March 18, 1963

I heard about a West Indian newspaper being published in Marseille and it arrived in my mailbox this morning, elegant and blue-toned. As I was flipping through it, Solange came running with a copy under her arm: "We have a newspaper! There's a list of 'eggheads' in it. According to those who wrote it, the only West Indian people in Marseille belong to high society. As for those slaving away, there's not a single line, not even to announce that they've departed this world . . . Read the 'Obituary' section, a comptroller of the treasury is the only person who died in the last six months, but we know Coppe went into the ground: on his way to buy coconuts this winter in La Joliette, he dropped like an anchor next to his shopping basket. And Guiche, the boatswain, who was always talking about the guy making this newspaper, he died in La Timone this winter: he only had three cats for company because he never showed off in a luxury car. Apparently he's not West Indian! And Use, who wasn't able to be a sales representative in the West Indies. She almost died near a pond at a lady's house, she's wasting away in a nursing home by Notre-Dame de la Garde, no one goes to see her. Isn't she West Indian? And Mamma Dede who polished so many parquet floors that rheumatism destroyed her shoulders! Have you seen those newspaper people visit her at Hôpital de la Conception? Are they ashamed to tell our chaplain that there are some among us who have fallen on "hard times"? He would go at least, the chaplain for West Indians, who is Provençal, to give them moral support. And Madame Marty who donned her madras when your newspaper people said 'olé olé'! Well, she goes from clinic to clinic, she also spent her life near Marseille's waters, she's crippled and who does she see besides her nurses? You turn a deaf ear, but it's too much. Look at this scam: 'The West Indian Circumference aims to provide moral and material support to compatriots in need, to the extent possible.' Well, I'm here to tell you that when those people see a West Indian with calloused hands and in need, they squash him immediately. I'm not just angry for the dead! But for all those who pay enormous dues to the association who don't receive a word of comfort in times of adversity. And they charge 250 francs for a punch. I'm not a member, but that's the cherry on top."

Of course, Carolina, I knew that Creole foolishness had reached Marseille, but Solange wouldn't let me get a word in, she was on a rampage. I knew that when the little West Indian maids came to find a bit of human warmth within the association, after slaving away for weeks in ladies' homes, the daughters of our leaders gave them such a "Nefertiti" look that they renounced any attempt at sisterhood. They tried the European dance halls instead.

I know! I know! And it upsets me. To know and not be able to do anything about it takes on a terrible significance in such moments. To calm my friend, I read her a delicious article from a newspaper I was sent from our country: "A Woman Transformed into an Ox."

A commotion in Saint-Esprit. Monsieur G. discovered a cow in his grocery store one morning, he was about to chase it away when it said to him: "Wait, I'm your wife, don't be angry." The husband, realizing that his wife was "under a spell," went to find the vicar.

Apparently the vicar gave the animal an injection, and after she had regained her human form, she was brought to Colson.* The disturbed husband ended up in the same place.

Solange cried:

"Impossible! What year was that written?"

"It's from last week," I said. "I took it from the mailbox just now."

Solange started to laugh as only she can. An infectious laugh, with a hint of mischief. She seemed to have forgotten the purpose of her visit. As I walked her back to the bus, she told me a thousand memories of the land, and the people rushing by in the violent wind stared at us, astonished.

I said goodbye to my friend, but I am not happy. Oh! Not the least bit proud. First things first, I'll go to the nursing home to see Lise and to Hôpital de la Conception to visit my mother Dodo, maybe that will ease my conscience! But what a scam that newspaper is.

Carolina, in times like this, I think of the underprivileged who are wrong to be so, in the eyes of imbeciles. I have to work hard to convince myself that I am not one of those imbeciles.

March 22, 1963

Solange came back, this time in her car; her husband is on vacation and the Citroën 2CV has left the garage: "Here

*A psychiatric hospital in Martinique.—Tr.

you go! I got you two tickets for the West Indian thing! Come check it out, it's worth it! They tell the Europeans that in our country there are only snack bars and villas with pools. It's worth the price and I want to gorge on their words. Tomorrow morning, if my boss is there too, I'll be able to tell her that none of it's true, that there are far more shacks than villas, far more people who wear three madras instead of two. The third, around their waist, they never show in 'your folklore.'"

As soon as there is something Solange doesn't like, she attributes it to someone: and so she attributes this folklore to me.

March 27, 1963

I finished my old lady's mending; her trousseau is ready for her to take to the nursing home. I visited the suffering, I consoled the crying! I racked up some good comments in my kids' notebooks, compensation for my extra hours spent making them read. So why not take advantage of Solange's offer to go see those who laugh and say that life is carefree?

There were lots of people at the party, the hall was packed to the brim. I joined the crowd and tried to spot an old West Indian philanthropist who lives in Toulon. The old man was there, leaning on his cane. He seemed surprised by the pomp of this gathering for which each family had to make sacrifices to afford the 30-franc entry fee.

There were speeches, Creole-style rice, punch, and madras.

The vicar of the West Indians and another erudite Provençal vicar told us charming, ad-libbed stories about the West Indies. And then other speakers, who had never used microphones before, waged frantic battles between their script and the sound equipment. In these moments, Solange kicked my feet under the table to catch my attention. And then the old man broached a subject more fitting for a church, a subject that everyone carefully avoids. He said: "All men are brothers, there should be no barrier between our skins, and perspectives on humanity should be subjects of conversation and not subjects of hatred." The wives of these gentlemen—who have West Indian women that they brought over to work fourteen-hour days—did not applaud. So Solange stood up and yelled "bravo!" Her husband yanked her dress to make her sit back down, she clapped her hands and said "encore!"

I was sitting between Solange's husband and a professor of something or other. It's horrible, those cunning minds that spew depraved stories! Of course, he didn't notice that I was embarrassed, my chocolate-colored ears don't turn red, and he didn't hold back!

I wasn't ashamed at not being cultured. What's the point of wasting time dissecting Voltaire and the rest to say such nonsense? But good grief, what must that idiot teach his students?

Solange was probably thinking the same thing. Solange looks ravishing: manicure, pedicure, hairdo, the whole shebang. If she weren't speaking in patois nonstop, she could have passed for Maria Montez!* She shrugged her shoulders

*Maria Montez (1912–1951) was a famous Dominican actress whose career tragically ended at the height of her stardom.—Ed.

and said, carefully pouring a bit of water into her wine: "He's really letting loose!"

The gentleman blushed and turned to face other guests!

Tonight, writing to you, Carolina, I say to myself: 10 kilos of oranges for 200 francs, that would make five packages for the sick West Indians who are in the hospital, sometimes with no visitors and no friends! I tossed and turned for a long time in my bed trying to fall asleep. Conscience is a thing that we should be able to put on or take off as we please; unfortunately it is entrenched in our bodies, and more than one person will be bothered by theirs tonight.

"Thou shalt rest sweetly if thy heart condemn thee not. Never rejoice unless when thou hast done well" (chapter VI of *The Imitation of Christ*). Remembering this, the day's events speak for themselves. The unabashed pride of some and the immense gratitude of others are swept away by these simple words.

March 28, 1963

While I was listening to the speeches yesterday and Cécile was watching my children (she refuses to go out before her fiancé has returned), my kids more or less behaved; it was raining, they weren't able to go for a walk in the countryside, as planned. They built rocket ships. It wasn't difficult. They took the cups drying over the kitchen sink and filled them with tin soldiers. The result was unsurprising: two or three rockets collided, and now my trash is filled with glass shards.

March 30, 1963

Finally, I can put away my boots and my muff. Slyly, on the edge of the road, little daisies thrust up toward the sun. In the courtyard of my little grandma's house, there is a lilac plant that was completely bare the last time; I glimpsed fat flies on its skeletal branches! I approached to observe this phenomenon up close and I spotted buds preparing to adorn the bush, despite the cold and this year's unending frost. I also saw a bird soaring through the sky: it might have been a swallow! Marseille is coming back to life, and women on park benches knit in the sun. I opened all the windows to welcome the first warm sun of the year and I turned off the heat. Carolina, I can't describe the effect that the changing of seasons has, it's an endless marvel for me, so used to a country without winter. I am happy to see people without overcoats enjoying the nice weather. When the pétanque players have taken out their boules, my joy will reach its apex, because this will mean that the season of cold winds is officially over.

Grandma couldn't believe it! I packed her suitcases, polished her kitchen, and I accompanied her on the bus to a nursing home near the Durance. She gave me a crocheted doily that she said she made herself. I couldn't refuse, it would have offended her. She assured me that she wouldn't forget me in her prayers, she was sincere. Her formerly blue eyes misted over with tears, I was emotional too. I turned around and cried: "See you soon! Six months go by quickly! I'll write to you!"

In that old white woman abandoned by her family I saw

my own mother who, in another land, might need help, support. On the bus home, I prayed: "Dear Lord, protect those I love from solitude and neglect."

March 31, 1963

Carolina, can I reasonably say that I wasted time because I didn't squeeze out all my juice in the home of a "lady"? No! I finished my first book, all that's left is to write the words "the end," but I can't bring myself to do it, an immense anxiety takes over me. When it wasn't yet a book, I could make every kind of conjecture; sometimes, I imagined people rejecting it, saying, "What a flop!"

Sometimes, I imagined it held in the hands of a "lady" practicing with her Marie-Chantal: "Oh! You can read! How wonderful."

Now that I'm finished with the book and with my conjectures, and now that I've written to the person who introduced me to you to ask for your advice, I feel embarrassed. It's hard to explain: did I have the right to mangle the language of Molière? Me, a poor negress? Did I have the right to say lovely things in bad French? That's what worries me! Participle agreement flies away right as I'm in the middle of constructing a sentence! And my eyes are worn out from late nights spent tapping away on my typewriter, and so there isn't a single line that doesn't contain some error. And the beautiful manner of speaking possessed by those fortunate enough to have studied literature, where does it run off to when I'm the one writing? Then I hear an immense clamor, bursts of laughter. The crowd says: What was she thinking, she only finished primary school! She's got some nerve! The clamor heightens, resounds in my head with such an intensity that I drop everything to go back to the world I never should have left. I wipe a kid's bottom, I peel my potatoes, and I think about finding a lady. This is my lot: I just have to stay in my lane and there won't be any issue.

I sent a letter to the *Match* journalist who wrote about you, like a castaway throwing a bottle out to sea, feeling hopeless. Luckily, spring is around the corner, and I will be so busy watching my city come back to life that my sad thoughts won't last long.

To build up my confidence as I wait for an unlikely response, I read my kids passages of my scribbling. Today, I read the chapter about the volcano, and my daughter started to cry: "It's too sad! Why is it so sad?" I didn't want to sadden her, I put my manuscript away.

The ashes of memories are not only the remains of joyous bonfires. There are also the embers of suffering, the pyres of spite, the twigs of tenderness and love.

My sons brought me their shoes busted open after an unruly soccer match. There will also be expenses for Cécile's wedding, and the family budget is in a real pinch. So I told my husband that I would find work, and he screamed his head off: "I don't want you working your fingers to the bone for some lady! Stay at home! Too bad about the wedding! Too bad about the busted shoes, they'll just have to wear them a little longer!"

When he flies off the handle, I tell him what he wants to hear, and then do what I want anyway. I went to the employment agency, the agent in charge of finding jobs for secretaries and bookkeepers told me I wouldn't find a half-time job. There's handling work, I could go to the chewing-gum factory, but I'd have to be there at 6:30 in the morning. So I checked the listings for "domestic servants." I didn't have much luck. The employee read me her registry: they only want people looking for "room and board." I am already roomed and boarded, so I went back home.

Chapter Eight

April 2, 1963

My son lost his history book. I went to the bookstore to buy him another. Surrounded by all those books arranged on their shelves, I got the idea to ask for information on how to publish a book. They are terribly nice, the booksellers, and nothing surprises them, since it's the season for April Fool's jokes. The first one I spoke to, at the end of La Canebière, was handsome, blond, well-dressed and distinguished. I told him that I had a friend who wanted to publish a book. He looked at me curiously, without laughing. Picture it, Carolina, I was carrying a net bag of provisions with chard leaves poking out. I don't know how he took me seriously, but the gentleman answered me sincerely: "Write to Gallimard, there's nothing in Marseille, and it's too bad, because people often ask me about this kind of thing!"

Write to Gallimard? I'm not crazy! He won't answer me. I didn't say that out loud, I simply asked for the history book. He didn't sell classics, so I bought a Mickey Mouse comic from him and got out of there. I went to Larousse, I spoke to a small, curt cashier with brown hair; I told him about my friend who wanted to publish a book, he asked me, "What kind of book?" and seemed interested. I explained, and the fateful words fell from his lips: "Nothing in Marseille! I also don't have the history book you're looking for. Tell your friend to make the rounds in Paris!"

Make the rounds in Paris? Hey, I hadn't thought of that!

I went to another bookstore on rue Longue-des-Capucins, near a funny hotel with dolled-up women standing outside. The bookseller was gray-haired and conscientious, he also didn't seem surprised; he had the book I wanted, I felt that I could speak openly, and I came right out with it: "I have a book I want to get published, what do I need to do?"

He took off his glasses and, despite the chard leaves bursting from my net bag to graze his windows, he said: "Well, that's wonderful! You should write to the Publishers Association in Paris, I don't know which arrondissement it's in, but it exists! A future writer in Marseille, that's great, that's great!"

He doesn't know what I've written, but he likes that there are writers in his city. Me too; I appreciated that. I walked back down the street, still dreary in this area, and I was convinced that this bookseller's words were not an April Fool's joke. My overly long chard leaves bothered me, I folded them back into the bag. For the first time in my life, I went to an employment office for cleaning women. In the manual labor offices, you have a choice of employment; in placement agencies for domestic work, there is no exhaust pipe. We know what awaits the women who go there.

I climbed up the six floors to the office. In the vestibule, six shiny wooden chairs for as many miserable skirts were already occupied by women hoping to find a job. The fine ladies in search of an employee don't sit alongside their future cleaning ladies; they take priority and enter the office without waiting in line. They look with open curiosity at those who are forced to wait.

A lady standing near me was waiting her turn to enter the

office; she smelled good, with manicured hands and a vulture's stare. She stared at me . . . stared at me with her cruel eyes. Fortunately the employees aren't auctioned off; she would have quickly taken me home with her. Finally she entered the office and asked the agent whether she knew me. The agent had never seen me before; she told the woman to wait and had me enter. The other women, who were there before me, grumbled.

There is no one sweeter than an employment agent! She strives to please everyone and win the trust of both employers and employees. I said right away that I was looking for a half-time job. She didn't ask for my documents or my name, I suited the lady with the hawk-eyed stare, that was enough.

The agent gently asked whether I could make myself available for the full day, lunch would be provided for me. Since I cook an outrageous amount for my brood, I have no interest in someone else's food. And I need at least half a day to take care of my own house, so I refused. The agent put on her best smile and told me that I was missing out on a golden opportunity. The lady left without a glance at me, she couldn't believe that I would decline her offer.

I had to explain to the agent that a ticket from her office assigning me an employer was indeed a kind of lottery whose advantages and risks I could accept, but I had seen that lady's eagle eyes and thin lips, and it wasn't worth getting involved with her.

"Oh!" she retorted, "you shouldn't judge by appearances!" And she gave me a half-dozen addresses in places so far from my house that I had to end my search for today. I didn't want to leave town empty-handed, so I went to a seamstress's shop and grabbed a large pile of brushed cotton pajamas to sew: for four francs per set, I'll have to work like a madwoman to make eight francs in a half-day. This will at least give me some time to find a lady I like.

And, Carolina, to fortify myself, I looked at the signs for a travel agency: I saw one advertisement for the Caribbean depicting languorous girls waving goodbye with their scarves. My soul burst into laughter as I pictured women dripping with sweat and carrying enormous bunches of bananas, or bent over in pineapple fields, or fastening piles of sugarcane without bathroom breaks, and my soul cried: "Go on and keep fooling yourselves, since life is one big fat lie."

I had to quiet my soul, I rearranged the chard in my bag and said aloud: "I need to get home and cook these things!"

A woman standing near me smiled, and my soul withdrew into its shell completely: there are far too many things to worry about now for my soul to be roaming around the West Indies.

April 8, 1963

My dear Carolina, I've only managed to sew four sets of pajamas in the last six days! I'm constantly being interrupted for various reasons, to find socks for my husband, to listen to my children recite their lessons, to chat with the neighbor or the mailman: it really wasn't smart to open a sewing shop in my house. I've just handed in my work and, desperate, I found myself back at the employment agency. The agent welcomed me by saying: "You're in luck, there's an opening across from your bus stop, by the zoo." I wrote down the address quickly; it was a blessing not to have to travel two kilometers to show up at a lady's house already out of breath.

The lady at the address hired me right away, without hesitation. She's elderly, with dyed hair. Her vestibule is a museum, her dining room a cafeteria, her kitchen a laboratory. She asked me if I knew how to cook. Is that a question you ask a mother? It's easier to learn than the proper table manners when there are three or four glasses or two or three knives. Still, it would be good if I could do an apprenticeship with an engineer so that I can use all the electrical appliances in her kitchen.

Besides, in this age when all the noblewomen want to be as skinny as asparagus, anyone can call themselves a chef. If you came to Europe, Carolina, you would see: you can't make anything with butter or salt pork fat! No puff pastries, no sauces to delight the nostrils! Carrots, leeks, skim milk, grilled meat galore, and in these kitchens made for cooking unctuous creams, fatty doughs, things that simmer! With food like this, why shouldn't I be a cook?

Right away, the little red-haired lady gave me a thick blue apron. I looked like a mechanic; she was pleased. She switched on her laboratory equipment. To grate six carrots, she brought out a machine with eight attachments that could have grated my fingers if I weren't paying attention. She had me perform the operation again to make sure I knew how because, she declared, I would be using it often.

In the time it took to do this meticulous work, I could have grated an entire kilo of carrots with a regular old knife. And then she showed me the appliance to make yogurt and the machine to toast bread. Next, she told me that I had to work five hours, from 9 a.m. to 2 p.m. These hours don't suit me at all, I would rather go home at noon. But there's the bonus of the nearby bus stop. I agreed.

April 10, 1963

My new lady said to me: "There are only two of us, you won't have much work," and then her daughter came back from her ski vacation with her two children: a seven-year-old kid, dull and impolite, and an adorable little doll who's two years old. The doll is sickly and disfigured, and if she were from my neighborhood, a legion of social workers would have already come by to find out whether she had been mistreated. To walk, she leans against the walls, and there's something sweet about this baby who tugs on my train-conductor blouse.

April 12, 1963

The first day I went to Madame's house, I brought a lunchbox. She said: "You don't need a lunchbox, this isn't a canteen! You'll always find something to eat!" So the next day, I brought nothing from home. Madame had said it was fine, but Monsieur looked at me, robust and sturdy with my 70 kilos, and said: "That woman must really eat!" That killed my appetite, and when I go back home at night, I'm quite hungry, because I hesitate to eat as much as I should.

April 13, 1963

Carolina! My pen will have a good laugh! Monsieur, who is a little old man with an expressionless gaze, came home with oysters. He said to me: "Madame, is there white wine in the fridge? I brought oysters!"

His wife answered for me with a categorical "No!"

Monsieur replied: "What about that local white wine, it will spoil, are we never going to drink it?"

After he left, Madame had me fill a small carafe with table wine and mumbled, "This will do!"

Monsieur came back, looked at me with his empty eyes, and said: "Do you like oysters?"

Madame answered without looking at me: "If she doesn't like them, oh well! There's still a tin of sardines from yesterday!"

Monsieur replied: "Does she like them or not!"

Insistently, Madame said: "Maybe she doesn't like them! The other Black woman never ate them!"

The other! But I adore seafood! To put them out of their misery, I said: "I prefer mussels!" I restrained myself from laughing my head off.

Monsieur immediately took the ball and threw it back to me: "But Madame, you'll eat with everyone! We'll go get you some mussels, won't we?"

Madame, beaming, said back: "You see, she doesn't like them!"

Good grief, I would have loved to try a couple of oysters, they were lying open there, looking succulent, but since I wasn't supposed to like them, I had to let it go!

April 13, 1963

In my blue uniform, I served up the meal without missing a beat. It's the first time this has happened to me and I enjoyed myself. To such an extent that I lost track of time as I was busy putting away my laboratory equipment. This pleased Madame and she deigned to smile.

April 14, 1963

Madame's daughter eats with the family today.

She is a leader, she has an authoritarian voice and the confident demeanor of those who want for nothing. On the telephone, she ordered a nanny, as if she were placing an order at the grocer's. She glanced at me suspiciously and noted to the governess, in charge of the personnel, that I understood French well. She added: "And her work? Is it just as good?"

The governess answered: "Yes! She's a quick worker, she could help the washerwoman!"

She turned to me and asked where I had learned to speak French.

I answered: "In Trinidad!" Likely not knowing where that is, she turned around and left!

I walked the equivalent of ten kilometers between the kitchen and the dining room. I hadn't yet put the food on the table, it's no joke, Carolina, especially when these people use an electric bell to call you.

I start to put away the appliances and suddenly a resounding DRINNNNNNG! makes me drop everything. Madame wants a plate, DRINNNG! the fiendish kid wants me to reheat his artichoke, but don't make it too hot! DRRRING and more DRRRRRRING. I come, I go, and I get distracted! I pass the salt when Monsieur wants the mustard and I have a constant urge to guffaw. Monsieur peeled a sorry-looking banana and said that it came straight from the West Indies! Bananas like that must come from Tenerife, not from the tropics. It can be amusing, but today my legs have had enough.

The governess came to tell me to hurry up and finish the dishes so that I could iron six sheets before I left; it didn't take much time, but I had to spray them and Madame's daughter doesn't like it when they're not completely smooth! And there I am sweating and panting so that every little corner of the sheets is as smooth as if they'd come out of a press. I didn't leave until three o'clock, but Madame said nothing about it!

April 15, 1963

I can't stand slacking off, so my schedule at Madame's house grows longer each day. Today the governess told me to bring the trash to the basement via the service staircase, which is narrow and winding. I don't mind, Carolina, but I have a little notebook where I write down all of my supplementary hours: there will be weeping and gnashing of teeth when it's time to pay up. In six days, I've accumulated five extra hours, and the governess seems particularly invested, as she's the one who keeps me from leaving on time for all sorts of reasons.

April 16, 1963

I was in the basement taking out the trash, a dim light illuminated my steps and a musty smell hung in the air. It was two o'clock and I was trying to remind myself that grown-ups don't get scared. As I was leaning over the bin, I had the unpleasant sensation of a presence behind me. Just under the staircase, there was a shadow. The time switch for the light went off and I heard a small creak. I jumped. I heard my voice resound in a strange monotone as I cried: "Who's there?" The shadow pressed the button and the blessed light dissipated my fear. A bleating voice answered.

"It's me, the concierge." In the shadows, I saw a skeleton in a woman's skin slowly advancing toward me. "I live here!" She pointed at the door to a cellar compartment!

Outside of Paris, I had never seen such a thing! "That's impossible," I said. She retorted: "And yet, it's true! I've been here for eighteen years! Just think, eighteen years with no sun, only artificial light, summer and winter! My husband died a while back, the canary in the cage, too! They were slowly suffocated by the gas that seeps in through the window. No plant can survive, and the flowers wilt as soon as I buy them!"

She leaned forward and scrutinized me: "But you're Black . . . like the other one who left. They'd made a room for her here." She pointed at another part of the cellar. "She didn't stay, poor thing, she was afraid of ending up like the canary. With all those cars giving off fumes just outside the window, it's understandable! Let me give you the tour!"

She opened the door. I had never seen anything sadder than that desolate room with no sunlight; a makeshift, dented bed, two wobbly chairs, misshapen furniture. She pointed at a hole near the ceiling covered in thick glass.

"I haven't opened it in a long time. When I do, too much dust gets in. My husband would open it after midnight, when there were fewer cars; that's how he got sick!"

"And your employers, what do they do for you?"

"Nothing, I'm retired now! Old-age pension! Before, I was the governess. When I got old, they put me here. I clean the building: it's all one family that lives here, cousins, friends. They bought the whole building! I do less and less work, I'm too old, they told me to go die somewhere else! I'm leaving after Easter for a nursing home. When I'm sick, I'm down here for days without any visitors. The other Black woman used to bring me herbal tea at night. Will you be living here?"

"Thank God, no! But who are your employers?"

"A bigshot down at the port! They're millionaires, you know!" Without resentment, the old woman added: "There have to be rich people and poor people, isn't that right? You know, you really shouldn't stay here. When I'm gone, they're going to put a maid down here. Think of the canary."

I emptied my trash can and sat on top of it. I would rather have the sky for my ceiling than this sordid dungeon. I told the old woman that I had a house under the pine trees, far from town. I told her that I had children who ran along the paths looking for wild plums, and how the almond trees had blossomed profusely this year in the Provençal countryside. And then I told her about my country. She listened to me eagerly, like a child being told a beautiful story. I forgot my employers and their kitchen. I told her that back home, even the hovels are drenched in sunlight! I spoke of the sun to help her forget all that darkness for a moment. I was down there for a while. When I returned, I saw the look on Madame's face—she was not at all pleased!

I told her that I'd had trouble closing the basement door. In any event, the twenty minutes that I spent down there are mine, I won't write them down in my little notebook.

It's unbelievable to discover such a thing in the cellar of

a rich person's home. I lost any desire to laugh. I was deeply disturbed to work for such individuals.

I told this to Cécile, who has left the biscuit factory; the seasonal work that she was doing is over now, so she's on a break.

Her break is filled with sweet anticipation for her nuptials, because she will be married soon, her fiancé arrives next week.

April 18, 1963

I can only write about my life as a cook at night, and sometimes I forget that I'm waiting impatiently for the mailman to bring me a response from the journalist I wrote to about my book. The children cruelly told me that he was probably dead, that real journalists report from incredible places! I consulted the latest issues of *Paris Match,* there wasn't anything announcing his death. This silence can be interpreted in many different ways. It could be a sign of boredom, a show of contempt, a moment of distraction, there are also silences heavy with hope or worry. In this silence which is my lot, there is no bitterness, nor even resentment, I am simply curious. If he wrote to me, "Dear Madame, you have written a flop," I would say: "Pfft! You might be right, but what displeases one person won't necessarily disgust others. Right now, my children gobble up my stories of sun and fruit, it's encouraging, it helps me to forget that it will be two weeks since I started working for this family."

Today, Monsieur brought home sea urchins. He looked at me with his expressionless eyes and said: "I'm going to open them! You don't like sea urchins, I assume?"

Immediately I retorted: "Yes, I do!" But in my head I was thinking, "Yuck!"

I've never liked those black sea urchins, all shells and spikes. When I would buy them in Fort-de-France, they weighed about 250 grams and they were brown; the black sea urchins in the West Indies were said to be venomous. The ones I've eaten over there had a taste somewhere between avocado and banana and smelled like the ocean.

I said yes to this villainous, gourmand little man just to see the look on his face.

Madame is the one who reacted: "Come on, sea urchins for the cook, you're not serious! And the ratatouille left over from yesterday, who's going to eat that?"

I had another good laugh! Monsieur said: "Since she likes them, I'll let her open them for herself." Brusquely, he threw six urchins on a plate for me. I opened those nasty little creatures and I placed them in a bag with pasta and the ratatouille and a bit of bread, on top of the trash, and as they were all enjoying their coffee, I went down to the basement to see the old shadow. I told her that this was the meal they had given me, that I would eat once I got home. She seemed frightened. She took the bread and the leftovers and told me to throw out the urchins, which didn't agree with her.

The sound of a voice brought me back to reality. The old woman said, "Go, quick! If she knows that you're talking to me, she'll fire you!" Carolina, to tell the truth, I would be happy to lose this job. Madame asked me to take the keys as I left: that way she won't have to come open the door for me. She scrutinized me and I couldn't lower my eyes, I wanted to say: "You should be ashamed to let your old maid turn into a ghost down there!" She looked away without questioning me.

April 19, 1963

Madame gave me two kilos of peas to shell. Her daughter, who was hanging about with no clothes on, said: "That's not enough, there are eight of us!"

Madame, pursing her lips, replied loudly: "No, five; the kids don't eat them and the 'others' don't count!"

By the others, she meant the nanny, the ironer, and me. This tactlessness made me want to explode. The young nanny had heard: on the balcony, she blushed all the way to the roots of her blonde hair and gave me a distraught look. I dropped the thing that chops carrots. I know Madame doesn't like for us to chuck the equipment, but she didn't tell me to leave.

Chapter Nine

April 20, 1963

The nanny left, blaming a high fever. This caught Madame's family off guard; they absolutely needed to have lunch in town, and it was the governess's day off, so they gave me a bright white apron and told me to watch the children. The kid made such a fuss that they took him with them, leaving me with the frail doe-eyed baby. Once they all left, the little sweetheart came scampering toward me. I put down my pots and took her in my arms. She nestled her little head against my shoulder as if she had always done so. I held the little thing who has such dreadful grandparents; the presence of innocents is a breath of fresh air in a hellhole like this. And then I had to add a vial of God knows what to her cold carrot puree poured from a carton that she had to choke down. She didn't want to eat, she was probably sick of those foods from dietitians and nurses. I used some laboratory equipment to grill two beautiful bananas that I bought at the local grocer's. I took a spoon and fed the little thing, who opened up her beak wide for this rare treat.

No drugs and no screams, she played and fell asleep while I sang her an old Creole song.

At two in the afternoon, the whole pack of them returned and her grandmother asked:

"Where is Évelyne?"

"She's napping," I answered calmly.

The baby's mother cried: "What's wrong with her? She isn't sick, I hope? Does she have a temperature?" She woke up the kid to stick a thermometer in her: the little thing who was sleeping so blissfully started to bawl, so much for her peace!

The grandfather thought to ask my secret for calming her down. If I had told him about the grilled bananas, he would have called the doctor to make sure the kid's stomach hadn't been perforated. Packed with vitamins, the little girl gurgled in the arms of her grandmother, who kept giving me strange looks. For the first time, she asked about my personal life: "You have a way with children, from what I can tell: this is the first time I've seen Évelyne happy after her meal! Do you have children?"

I couldn't believe it! She had never given me a name up to now, she's always used her bell: twice for the Black, once for the governess. I couldn't believe it! She asked my name! I told her it was Jacqueline! I could have just as easily said Renélise or Pierrette, I'm sure she'll never ask for my paperwork. Unless I decide to declare myself to social security and I give them to her myself, but until then . . .

The euphoria would have lasted if the fiendish little boy hadn't kicked me right in the leg.

I forgot that the family wanted to know my name and I threatened the kid with a smack. He had never heard that kind of threat in his life, he stared at me, shocked, as shocked as his grandmother, who, once more, pursed her lips. The grandfather, on the other hand, conceded: "It's true, we'll have to start punishing him if he's going to attack the maids."

Carolina, no one told him that it was naughty, I could tell

he wanted to give me another kick. But he won't try with me, he wouldn't dare, anyway . . .

April 21, 1963

I did not smack the little boy in the end and they have still not managed to digest that I had the audacity to threaten him! . . . As I was doing my daily jog from the dining room to the kitchen, Madame's daughter, deliberately ignoring my presence, said: "What were you thinking, hiring this Baker? Did you notice, she doesn't even wear her apron anymore! The other one would never have dared threaten Gilbert with a slap! Now we've really seen it all!"

She wasn't speaking to me, and I didn't get involved, I was too busy passing the salt, heating up the pasta, cooling down the roast.

My soul surfaced again and said: "Keep it up, belle Madame! If your kid hits my shins again, you'll see what I'll do to his bottom: two good smacks on each cheek, that'll put him in his place!"

Carolina, how wonderful it is to hear that inner voice and know that, when we want, we can act on it! It was so pleasant that I didn't even hear the family's excessive, imperative DRINNGs.

And then I thought of "the other one," who wouldn't have dared. What dreary place did she come from? What boat inadvertently left her in France and what ill fate brought her to these recalcitrant people? And when I'm gone, there will be "another," just like the "other" who preceded me, and I have no idea when it will stop.

The little thing got out of her chair and scampered over

to me, she refused to eat her mush, she stared at me, I knew that she was thinking about her lunch from the day before; I didn't dare take her in my arms, I would have been so upset if the grandmother noticed and, hopping mad, sent her tumbling down with a cutting remark.

I met Cécile's fiancé, he doesn't want to delay his wedding by a week. He's here and he wants to marry right away, he went to speed up the formalities at the town hall, and Saturday he'll walk down the aisle with our wise Cécile.

Cécile wants to help me, she told me that I have talent, she dug up the address of a literary agent and wrote him a long letter in her best handwriting. It's nice to have a secretary, all I have to do is sign my name and that's that. Cécile said: "I can't believe you don't stay at home to write heaps of things!"

That's a wonderful idea, but, as my husband says, you can't toss paper with salad dressing. I'll see what this literary agent has to say: I just hope he won't stay silent like the *Match* journalist! That would put an end to the pipe dreams of my little world.

April 30, 1963

Ever since I barged in with a beautiful nylon apron and relegated Madame's blue coveralls to the closet, I knew I would not be forgiven for this high treason, and I wondered what she would do to make me feel her wrath. Today, she told me that she was taking over her laboratory and that I would be scrubbing and repolishing the rooms. Six rooms, 42 square meters each! To scour centimeter by centimeter in order to remove a wax that's been stuck there for half a century! Since the time of the dodos! My sweat was dripping over those slabs, resistant to even the most heavy-duty steel wool! I did a quick calculation: 252 square meters of parquet floor in four hours. A thousand francs for four hours! .25 francs per square meter of vigorous work! It was too little! I folded up my nylon apron and asked Madame to pay me what she owed: it was good timing, because it's the end of the month. Do you think, Carolina, that she was happy to see me leave? She asked for her eight days' notice. I work on a day-to-day basis, according to my desire and my needs; I didn't give her the time to say it again. I replied: "Not another second, or else I'll have a stroke." I was really angry: for the first time, she saw my rage. She was afraid that I would fall ill, but she was still determined, she withheld eight days of pay. I was angry, but I knew how to count, I even demanded the extra hours that I had accumulated; if she refused, I would go to the labor inspection office, which exists for my sake too, after all! I knew too many things for Madame's liking, she needs Blacks who come straight from the bush, who've never heard of social laws. She paid me and let me go.

I said goodbye to the old woman in the basement and took off, happy, happy never to see them again.

Even so, I take with me the image of the little girl nestling her innocent head on my neck, and that woman with no family and no friends, living in a cellar with no sunlight, in the home of heartless people.

May 1, 1963

It's International Workers Day and there are lilies of the valley everywhere, even ones made out of plastic. Those will last a long time, and the delicious wait for this beautiful month will lose its meaning because each day those odorless sprigs will be there to remind them that May once was.

We're getting ready for the wedding here, everyone has their dress clothes. There is sun everywhere, and I pity those who can't take the time to enjoy it.

May 3, 1963

Solange came in her 2CV to lend me a hand. My kitchen is no laboratory, but how wonderful it is to make things by hand, coconut cakes, puff pastries; Solange learned how to make pizzas from a Corsican, paella from a Spaniard, and spring rolls from a Chinese restaurant. She babbles, she bustles. She is leaving, she says, to "rise up in the ranks"; that makes us laugh as only we can.

"I'll go punch some tickets in the metro, since Defferre won't bring the metro to Marseille! If you could see how many negresses work in the metro and in the hospitals there! I've even seen them in the department stores in Paris! 'They' take it to heart that the West Indies are French territories and they accept that West Indians can be something other than maids. On that note, my children, there's a negress who's just arrived in Marseille: you must go see her! She works in a large butcher shop on rue Longue-des-Capucins. You won't believe the line in front of her stall! Everyone wants to see if she knows how to weigh properly, if she knows how to say, 'Will that be all, madame' or 'Who's next?' The poor thing, she never stops, and all the proud negroes go buy from her!"

Solange is irresistible and everything is rosy when she speaks. She looked at my hands dubiously and said: "Take care of your nails, good grief! Be careful, your fingers will turn into sausages if you let those ladies' products irritate your skin like that." I was ashamed of her observation and stopped typing the grocery list for my kid. It's terrible, hands busted like old elastic, fingers swollen from going straight from a hot tub of water to a freezing basin. In these ladies' homes you can't say, "I just ironed, my hands are hot, I'll wash the sink tomorrow." It's precisely when you've just worn yourself out in an overheated kitchen that the women who pay you 250 francs per hour feel the need to have you rinse the lingerie that can't be washed in warm water. Sometimes I say: "My God, let her experience poverty for a week! Just one week, to make her more sympathetic." Well, Carolina! I hid my fingers! Even if our morale is unscathed when we do these jobs, what a hit our bodies take! You have to be like Solange, always on your guard! She claims that by going to make little holes in metro tickets, she'll keep a nice physique for a long time. Cécile is radiant, she listens to Solange as she cuts a mountain of pain de mie into small squares. She invited a few young people from the biscuit factory, and her fiancé invited a few friends from the military. I pushed the furniture aside to make room for dancing, and I put flowers everywhere: and so I give my home a festive atmosphere.

May 5, 1963

They are married! The whole neighborhood lined up on the church parvis! Cécile was beautiful in her white dress;

a spectator said rather loudly: "I didn't know gowns suited Black women so well! See how good they look?" We looked more than good! I would even say we looked elegant! I wore long gloves because I couldn't stop thinking about Solange's comment, and my hat was a big hit! Solange had the poise of a great lady, and the others proved that they weren't West Indian in name only! All their lives they had worn nothing but sundresses, and on this May day it was only natural for them to don those dresses once more! And all those handsome men invited by the fiancé made more than one woman who claims not to like negroes swoon. Solange told me that as we climbed into her little car with two of my children. And then we danced, we forgot the ladies, we forgot our bitterness. We thought of nothing but the happiness of Cécile, who spoke of going back to our country as soon as possible. And then she packed up and left in the night. This morning, there's nothing left but empty bottles, languishing flowers, and the remnants of the feast to remind me that from now on, she's a part of the past.

May 6, 1963

Cécile had been bold enough to write and it yielded an unexpected result: the literary agent answered me. On the beautiful envelope with the company's logo, he typed: "Maméga, woman of letters." I sat down on the doorstep, my legs buckling with emotion, and I reread those words, "woman of letters," I rubbed my eyes to make sure I wasn't seeing things. It was really written there: "Maméga, woman of letters." I called the children: "Come quick! Look what's written on this envelope!" One of them read it and asked me who I had made letters for. I didn't correct him, I just said: "For a man! Look what's inside!"

Surrounded by my brood, I awaited the literary agent's negative verdict. He had probably written "woman of letters" to give me the courage to stomach the rest: "You are an imbecile," or something along those lines. But then my kid started to read and I had to tug on my ears, Carolina, to make sure they were really mine, as the little one said: "Madame, I read the excerpts of your manuscript with great pleasure, and I eagerly await the rest. So much poetry and real charm emanates from these pages." The youngest was reading, the others listening. The letter was all praise and encouragement. The agent ended with these words: "The errors in this text should be corrected in order to present it to a publisher . . . "

My daughter said: "He's buying your book!"

One of her brothers jumped for joy and said: "So, you won't have to go to ladies' homes anymore, and we'll get to meet Mama Doudou!"

Isn't it the dream of all transplanted children to meet their grandmother? Most of them never knew her, or will never know what it means to have an aunt or an uncle of their own, and when their classmates casually mention going to their grandmother's house or outings with their grandfather, they feel frustrated. I always tell them: "When we have enough money, we'll go to Grandmother's house!"

Maybe you won't believe me, Carolina, but each time I've amassed some savings, it melts away like snow in the sun, because Easter blooms and I don't want my little Martiniquans born in Marseille to be less spring-like than the others, or Christmas arrives just as I've paid off their new school clothes. It doesn't upset me, because this is the case for many more families than people think. But what pains me is when my family asks about Grandmother: "What is Mama Doudou like? Does she have white hair?"

I describe her little house under an enormous plum tree, her hens that peck at your feet. The eldest told me to bet on horse-racing. I never do, because it's too hard to win a few francs, I don't win, but I don't lose either. So now I tell them: "When I've written an entire library of books, I'll have enough money and we'll go see Grandmother."

Today, I'm on the first book of my library and my children are already thinking about Grandmother. There was something comical about it, Carolina, we were all there on the doorstep, forgetting to enter the house, too eager to devise this lovely plan, the children wouldn't let me budge. And then papa arrived, he leaned his moped against the plane tree on the side of the road. The children swarmed him and yelled: "We're going to Martinique to see Mama Doudou!"

Imperturbable, he answered: "Is that so! If it's not Santa bringing the caravel this time, what is it?"

They all wanted to be the one to tell him, the letter, the man who wrote the letter, the things written in the letter!

He didn't miss a beat; he said to me: "How much will it cost you to publish your scribbling! Did you think of that?" And to the children: "You should all be thinking about finding good jobs, if you want to pay for the publication of your mama's book! In the meantime, enough messing around."

His words were like a cold shower. And it's a good thing, because there is an entire world between dream and reality.

May 8, 1963

Carolina, I wish you could see how marvelous Provence is, despite the nasty ladies one meets here! People talk of serious matters in a sonorous tone, with a smile that always makes me happy, even when, like today, I am down in the dumps. I keep asking myself how I could ever get enough money to pay a publisher, since it's expensive to publish a book. I hadn't even thought of that. At noon I wondered: "How can I manage it without going to work for a lady for a long time?" It's a problem. A woman knocked on my door, she had eyes as clear as the sky. She was carrying a large bundle of newspapers. I thought she was a saleswoman distributing flyers at first, then that she was trying to sell me a vacuum. I didn't slam the door in her face because she had a confident smile, and you should respect people's confidence. I tried to tell her that I had enough brooms and that she could come back another day for the vacuum. I couldn't get a word in. She handed me a sheet of paper and told me that she came in the name of God! Nothing more! Since we should always do everything in the name of God, I was willing to hear what she had to say. Well, she assured me that God lived in Provence, in Montfavet! I knew that God was roaming around here because this morning, on Avenue des Trois-Lucs, I picked so many lilacs, when just a few days ago nature was still being timid! And to fight against my blues, the sun enters through all the windows of my home so fiercely that it's enough to reinvigorate even the saddest among us! So it might well be true that God lives in Provence more so than in Finistère. And yet it's bizarre that He comes to vacation here when there are so many things to do in the world. I said this to the smiling woman. She answered that God was alive and well, that He lived near Avignon. She rolled the ends of her words, which seemed a bit farcical. I laughed harder than Saint Thomas, so much so that I had to sit down to catch my breath. Of course, I wasn't mocking her, because I listen gladly to those who speak of God, it's a change from my usual conversations. To excuse my sudden gaiety, I invited her to sit, and I asked her what He was like, the Good Lord who lives in Provence. She wasn't fazed and, illuminated by an inner fire, she replied that I had until the year 1963 to repent and listen to the voice of God, along with the other inhabitants of the Earth. After that, chaos would erupt!

Let it come! I'm not afraid of the afterlife! I'm creating my afterlife now in my present, through my sweat, my tears, my forgiveness. Is it arrogant to say this to a woman so sure of herself? But I wanted to challenge her. A person's afterlife, I am convinced, can be horrendous or radiant, no matter their rank or their race. I said this to the lady, without laughing, and I added: "But, really, I can't quite believe that God is so close by and I haven't dropped everything to follow Him, that He's so difficult to detect, so close to Marseille! My God with the scarred face, the impaled feet, ribs dripping with disgrace, I would recognize Him from a mile away. He is here, but we can't see Him yet. He is crushed in the dust, we trample Him, and He cannot yet rise. But when He does! Blessed are those who can say then: 'Come what may!'"

The woman listened to me raptly, curiously, astonished. And then she told me that the god in Montfavet is a mailman at the post office! Carolina, I burst into laughter again and I renounced my prophesies.

My great visionary left me some newspapers and offered to order me miraculous books, because He is also a printer and a shopkeeper just like any old guy, that God of Provence! Oh! What a tall tale!

Chapter Ten

May 15, 1963

"Since the literary agent asked for my scribbling, why not send it to him?" I said to myself. "He will read it in full and then I'll find out how much he'll charge me." No sooner said than done, I bought a nice folder and put my pages inside. Registered mail, please! I wouldn't want my pages handled carelessly, with all the unimportant mail. You see, Carolina, I'm becoming pretentious!

Women of letters, I imagine, have offices with proper lights. Sound doesn't penetrate their sanctuaries. I write to you by the light of the large bulb in the kitchen while the children endlessly recite their lessons for tomorrow. But I know you are less privileged than me, with only a gas lamp in a favela, so I tell myself: "You're lucky, you old hag! Why are you making excuses?" And so now I've started on the first pages of my second book, because I can't wait to be a millionaire to write a second one, that might take too long; like the farmer's sons, I dig, I search, I dig some more: surely I will find the buried treasure with a bit of patience and willpower.

I have to think ahead to summer: I flip through the newspapers, I comb through the classified ads to find a job that doesn't require a full day outside, but not in a lady's home. After buying the winter clothes, now I have to think of the bits and bobs for vacation; I promised my kids to bring them to Paris, which is being cleaned at the moment. What more beautiful trip for children raised among the pine trees than a visit to Paris in the middle of summer, when everything is calm and the Champs-Élysées is host to only a few tourists! Of course, I'll have to earn enough to pay for the cost of travel, at least, so newspapers are piled up in my house, I dive into all the job offer columns. I saw: "Doctor seeks West Indian maid." I also read: "Chewing-gum factory seeks young woman for simple tasks."

I went to the chewing-gum factory near my house. You have to be there at seven in the morning, because half-time work is nonexistent in the large companies of the region. I continued my prospecting and I found the following announcement in a newspaper: "Hôtel de l'Arrivée seeks seamstress, four half-days per week."

May 17, 1963

I went to Hôtel de l'Arrivée, near Marseille's Harlem: on the doorstep were many pretty dolled-up and scantily clad women. I asked to speak to the owner; one of them said, insolently:

"What for?"

"For the seamstress job!"

The woman shrugged her shoulders and said: "Jeez, another one! Five women have come by and she hasn't liked any. Go on and try your luck!"

I crossed the narrow hallway and went to the front desk. An imposing woman of color scrutinized me sternly.

"If you're looking for a room, we're full!"

"No, it's for the seamstress job!"

"You know how to sew?"

"Yes, what kind of sewing?"

She didn't answer me and continued to look at me probingly.

"The job is a bit unusual, I'm not looking to hire a seamstress who will cause problems. It's two weeks, no social security, and I can find you work afterward because all the hotels around here need a seamstress. You'll be cutting the used sheets in half and turning the fabric inside out so we can keep using them. It's been two years since I've had this done, I have a closet full of them! Are you West Indian?"

"Yes!"

"I'll give you priority if you agree to work without social security."

I wasn't going to quibble over social security when she was offering me three francs fifty per hour, more than the ladies and more than the factory, where you only make two francs twenty-five; on top of that, I get a ten-stop bus ticket each day for my commute! I said yes: I begin tomorrow.

May 18, 1963

The hotelier set me up in a large empty room with a sewing machine, thread, and a mountain of sheets. Through the glass door, I could see the ladies coming and going with men all morning, it went on for a while. And I left without seeing the owner again. A woman came to ask me for a needle and thread because a button on her blouse had come off, and she added: "Nasty work, huh! It's so dusty in here! Make sure you're paid well, the manager earns plenty of money!"

May 19, 1963

There are more sheets than I thought, and the more I cut, the more I rush, the more they pile up. When the hotelier is absent, the women come talk to me. One is breathless and skinny like a model, she enters the room, pushes the pile of sheets off the chair and collapses into it: "Phew! I need to rest for a minute! I'm tired of working."

I was immediately curious about what kind of work she does, but I would never dare broach the topic. Since she said she was tired, I asked her why she was still working here; whether she had a house, a family?

"I'm married, my husband is the one who got me the job here!"

I was appalled and frantically busied myself with my work.

May 22, 1963

There is a constant back-and-forth of women and I only see the hotelier when she takes the finished sheets. Today, she let me know that she was "from the colony." She didn't need to tell me; she still has the trade wind blowing through her accent. I suspect she's from Pointe-à-Pitre or Fort-de-France.

May 23, 1963

Today, a frantic gallop broke up the monotony, women running down the corridor like lunatics. I think they were fleeing from a police inspector making his rounds in the area. One of them said: "He's a pervert! He changed his hat and did you see where he parked his car, the wrong way in the middle of a one-way street! Luckily Juliette spotted him in time! I had to ditch a good client!"

The little woman who was worn out the day before added: "It scares the daylights out of me every time and now I'll be sick for two days!"

The owner yelled: "Shut up! Sit down in the sewing room and find something to mend!"

I looked at those women with their hair styled like artichokes, tapping their voluminous hairdos, polishing their manicured nails, glancing disapprovingly at the heap of mending piled up in the room.

The hotelier turned around, grumbling: "With wimps like them, I'll never get by! They take off every time one of those pigs runs across the sidewalk! I'll have to hire other 'employees.'"

The girl who seemed to be the leader of that strange group said: "Employees! We're the ones who pay you, aren't we? Five hundred francs a trick, and you would rather go without eating, without even leaving to buy groceries, for fear that we'll sneak one by you!"

The owner wasn't hard of hearing, she turned back around and yelled: "How about you shut your mouth? All you do is complain! Enough!"

The woman went quiet. A heavy silence hovered over

the dusty room. One of the women carefully peered through the curtain and announced that the scare was over: "Adèle is over there laughing it up!"

Across the street, there were other hotels and other girls: if those women were outside, the ones involuntarily keeping me company could be out there, too. There was a joyous stampede down the hallway as the hotelier looked on ruthlessly. And there you have it. Until we've seen it with our own eyes, Carolina, it's hard to believe that this voluntary slavery exists.

May 26, 1963

My husband came to meet me tonight, I saw him enter at the same time as the hotelier informed me he was there:

"So, you didn't tell me this place is full of hussies!"

"Hussies? I see nothing but my sheets and I work like a slave, the rest is none of my business."

I hadn't spoken to him about the ambiance of my workplace: he would have forced me to end my tenure there a long time ago. And we can only properly speak of what we've seen.

The hotelier let me leave, I hoisted myself onto the back seat of the moped and clung to my absolutely furious husband. The wind soothed my face and my thoughts, and I didn't even notice that my driver was not taking the little side roads to avoid motorcycle cops as he usually did. It's true, I surpassed the fourteen-year age limit for riding on the back of a moped a long time ago.

He plunged through the cars, threading the lanes with incredible dexterity, zooming at full speed down the avenues, proof that he was really angry; in such moments, better to let him blow off steam than to pick an argument, and besides, he wasn't entirely wrong to be upset.

And then we found ourselves on rue Saint-Pierre in the direction of Saint-Marcel. Two motorcycles raced by at more than 80 kilometers per hour. I cried: "Highway patrol! They didn't see us, we're lucky!"

We had been driving in the opposite direction of the motorcycles for another good ten minutes when the sound of their engines made me turn my head. They were heading straight for us! It wasn't worth trying to get out of it, by pretending to reinflate a tire, for example. They had already spotted us.

My husband stopped his engine and the motorcycles reached us. I looked at the patrolmen, they were darker than Moors; booted, belted, helmeted, they seemed gigantic in the impending, violet dusk. One of them began the standard routine: "License and registration!"

The other said to me: "Don't you know you shouldn't be sitting on the back of this vehicle?"

I answered: "No, Monsieur!"

He looked like a handsome mechanical toy and I thought: "For Christmas, I'll buy some biker figurines at the general store for the kids, they're pretty impressive!"

During that time, my husband managed to talk his way out of the ticket.

"I don't live far from here. This doesn't happen often! I'm very careful."

The police who had examined his paperwork reprimanded him: "You say you have children! But you risk not making it home to them!"

"Madame, go to the stop to wait for your bus and do not get back on that moped!"

It wasn't negotiable: in any case, there was nothing to say. I headed for the deserted bus stop and under the surveillance of those unexpected angels I saw my husband disappear around the bend toward La Valentine. Twenty minutes after the patrol had vanished toward the south—I imagined they had gotten on the highway—I was still waiting for my bus when a roar accompanying two black dots to the north informed me that those shrewd men had made a detour and then circled back to see if I had disobeyed their order. Instinctively, I waved hello. One of the limited-edition toys slowed down and, with a quick hand motion, returned my greeting.

I got back home quite late. My husband's patience had run out, what with the motorcycles, my madness at working anywhere I pleased, and the ladies of the night who would contaminate me. "Things are going to change! You will stay home: bringing back a few coins isn't going to change our circumstances!"

But, Carolina, it's so nice not to say: "When my husband brings home his paycheck, I'll buy myself a pair of stockings!"

I need to convince him that I am off limits in my dusty room, and that they recently installed a curtain over the window on the door to shield my gaze. And that above all, it's only temporary. For me, everything must be temporary, apart from my brood and my notebooks that I fill up hastily everywhere I go.

May 28, 1963

Phew! I was able to leave again and I have almost finished my job: the hotelier, because of my steady silence, was less standoffish today, she came to ask if I liked working here and offered me coffee. She finally spoke to me in patois and even told me things in confidence: "It's tedious to manage a place like this, you have to keep your eye on everything! I can't hire a security guard, I don't trust them. I'm alone! My husband abandoned me for a white! Since then, I've made it on my own and I show him what the whites do around here! They'll even sleep with bums as long as they have cash! It disgusts me, but I have my revenge!"

It was abominable, Carolina, to hear all that! I saw the frightened little woman fleeing in fear of a vice squad raid! And the fat girl whose buttons are always flying off, who leaves stuffed with money at night, and by the morning she's so broke that her coworkers buy her breakfast. I know the innate faith of Black people, I said to her in Creole:

"Aren't you afraid that God will punish you?"

"God! He forgot about me a long time ago! I was working as a housekeeper in 1939 in Paris, I was seventeen years old! My bosses fled while I was sleeping on the sixth floor, and when I woke up, there were Nazis searching for them! They didn't kill me. They raped me and beat me. So, God . . . "

I wanted to scream; I was looking at this monstrous woman and tears were running down her face, swollen by sleepless nights, I had endless pity for her. I didn't talk about it when I got home that night. My husband asked: "How many more days are you going to work there? Look what I brought you, paper for your typewriter, a ream of a thousand sheets, and I got your typewriter from the pawnshop! Write if you're bored, type up the words of *Little Red Riding Hood* if you're short on ideas, but stop going to that street. If people we know saw you over there!"

People! I don't care, Carolina, there are things we must dare to do, and in less than a month I've learned more than I could have from a mountain of books!

June 2, 1963

Ah! I'm done with the job and I'm sick with disgust again. The hotelier was kind, she gave me a bonus and the address of two of her friends who have hotels who would hire me to do some sewing. But I couldn't manage to look her in the eyes when I left, I felt too ashamed about what I had witnessed that afternoon.

I've never been surprised by the presence of a certain young boy in this establishment because the upper floors are occupied, unfortunately, by families. I was convinced that his parents lived here, hence his comings and goings through this hallway. And then a girl returned from the laundry room in a rage as I was in the middle of transforming the used bath towels into gloves.

She yelled: "Give me one of those old towels for this little shit! The owner isn't here, we'll end up having to go somewhere else! We are honest! We can't work peacefully anymore, there are always young kids competing with us. If my son ends up turning tricks like this, I'll strangle him with my own hands! I pick up men, why doesn't he just pick up women!"

The curtain was open, I saw a gentleman waiting. The girl passed a towel with holes in it to the young man, who followed the gentleman. I thought that these things only happened in adult films, and then here we are, in the middle of May, while on La Canebière, a stone's throw away, hundreds of women walk around, each more beautiful than the last, offering an embarrassment of options to even the pickiest of men! A young boy, a child who could have been anyone's son, furtively entered a seedy hotel for the most horrid reason! My pity for this atrocious woman vanished and I was ashamed to be of the same race! Good grief, she needs to leave that to someone else! . . .

I thanked the hotelier for her offer to help and said goodbye. I ran like mad to the Church of the Reformed, I used my bonus, which was burning a hole in my pocket, to place altar candles in front of all the saints. I hurried home, I glued images I had cut out of sports magazines over the boys' beds, pictures of Anquetil and Rummel, of Sainte-Rose and Kopa. They were delighted, but I'm still haunted by the thought of the kid at that hotel.

Chapter Eleven

June 5, 1963

Nine years since my husband left the army! Nine years he's been waiting for an "emploi réservé" in his region! They did already offer him a job as a forest ranger in Allier, a mailman in the Bas-Rhin, a railroad worker in Brittany, a warden in Le Havre. But we love Marseille and its sun; in the summer, we'll see the whites turn black on the charcoal grills that are our beaches, it's amusing and only ten tram stops from our house! So, why go to Bas-Rhin? West Indians haven't gotten on board with skiing yet, that's only in the movies. Here, we can always find a pine tree to camp under with the kids, and there are rocky inlets surrounded by a sea so azure that I have to remind myself: "In the West Indies, the sea is also incredibly blue." For all these reasons, we won't move. My husband, who has just been offered a new position through the "emploi réservé" system, left to find someone to "pull some strings."

Indeed, like every self-respecting Provençal, he thinks that "going to Paris" will sort things out. This time they've offered him a job as a security guard in a national museum in the capital. He'll go ask whether there's a vacant position in a museum in Marseille, to avoid the move and especially the lack of sunlight. He will be gone for four days to visit a ministry. It's quite nice, when we're far away, to say: "I'll go to such and such ministry." It typically doesn't yield any results, but we still have the satisfaction of being there. I said none of this to him, but I took advantage of his trip to Paris; I asked him to go in person to *Paris Match* to get an update from my journalist. I carefully cut out the address from an issue of the magazine and gave him a letter for the editor-in-chief. Perhaps the journalist, poor man, is dead, or he has no secretary! Which would make it difficult for him to answer me. But the editor-in-chief, if I understand how things work, must have a heap of clerks that he can task with answering correspondents. Of course, the letter mentions the few pages I sent to the journalist. Those few pages were precious to me, Carolina, I excerpted them from my book. Imagine, I amputated my text; now I have to type everything up again. My husband told me that you can't just waltz right into *Match,* but since he's "heading up there," he'll do me the favor of delivering my letter.

June 6, 1963

Today is my shopping day. When it's nice out, my husband tows me to the market, but even if he were here he wouldn't take me this time, he's too afraid of running into the patrol. Riding on his moped is always relaxing for me, the mistral whips my face and rejuvenates my skin. I have my own bike, but I haven't been able to ride it since a prankster stole one of its wheels while it was parked in a lot downtown. Now I have to cross the ten kilometers that separate me from the city by bus, which is rather banal, and when it's nice out, I have to line up to wait for the bus, when I'm used to doing the opposite! Habit, I can confirm, makes slaves of those who "get used to" it.

I met a woman from Guadeloupe who has seven children and came to France to receive the same benefits as the French in this country. It worked. Her husband goes to the docks from time to time and she lives in a hovel until they can afford something better. She feels happy even so, because with her benefits she considers herself a full citizen; thus, she told me, when her boys go off to fight in the next war, she won't have the impression that that's all they're good for. She told me to come to the market after five tonight, that they sell meat at an incredible price at a vanguard butcher shop on rue Longue-des-Capucins. It would be worth the trip, she assured me. All the in-the-know housewives would be there.

I left this afternoon with one of my boys and met my compatriot, who also had two children in tow. She drove me to the establishment where the sale would take place. A woman said: "I hope Ernest doesn't start the 'bada' sale late like last week." I glanced around; all the destitute of Marseille were gathered there, as well as many curious people who had come to watch. I tried to blend in with the curious but my compatriot called to me and advised that I stand my ground near the front: otherwise I wouldn't get a good bundle.

Ernest auctions off the meat: all the leftovers from the huge butcher shop where he works are transported to the back room that opens onto a street behind the establishment. He calmly sets up his stall. From time to time, an apprentice brings him a tray of various, unidentifiable pieces of meat. In the blink of an eye, the crowd had significantly expanded, and I had to keep pushing my kid forward so that he wouldn't be trampled. Ernest has no scale or weight. He makes heaps of things from the scraps they bring him for five francs per heap. He began with inedible plates of mutton ribs mixed with a few pieces of rank merguez. The people in a hurry took these bundles. My compatriot told me that, until he finished selling what I thought was mutton, he wouldn't move on to other things. Then Ernest yelled: "Now for the pot-au-feu! Whoever takes the pot-au-feu will get some bada!"

Bada, I learned, is a smidgeon of beefsteak that Ernest generously places in his bundles. When he made this announcement, there were more hands than bundles to sell. Ernest knows his customers, he gives them veal blanquette or some kind of roast that isn't too blue for the same price of five francs. Seeing those prime bundles riled up the crowd, who shouted: "Come on, Ernest, you're leaving me hanging? I'm next!"

Ernest doesn't know which way to turn his head, which is adorned in a checkered hat. The men are dogged, and they forget the gallantry that should compel them to cede their place to the women. This is a matter of the stomach, Carolina, and taking home an edible bundle is a victory for those who've waited more than an hour.

Ernest stopped to cut and wrap pieces of things, and suddenly he shrieked: "Mesdames! Be careful, there's no pickpocket, but there is the same pervert from last Saturday who chased away my customers. It's the creep in the back! He will grope you! That's why he comes here. You've been warned!"

I looked at the creep who turned completely red and left without asking for a scrap, because all the women threatened him with kicks of their sharp heels or whomps with their shopping bags. My compatriot said to me: "You see why it's worth it to come early? The perverts always look for a crowd to slip in among the buyers!"

Then Ernest grabbed two large plates of inedible things from under the counter; he made piles and yelled again: "So! The price hasn't gone up, it's still five francs a pile, the price of a pack of cigarettes! Still no takers for the top round! Well, I'll add in some bada!" A few hands reached out lazily. Ernest wasn't satisfied with the showing; he crossed his arms and threatened to leave with the trays of entrecôte he'd just been brought if he couldn't manage to get rid of the bundles he had already prepared.

That didn't work, so Ernest mixed everything together: the entrecôte, the scraps, and the remaining merguez, he even cut slices of roast beef to spruce up the piles. Delighted, he adjusted his cap and wiped his hands on his long apron: "Now, don't say I didn't spoil you!"

My compatriot said: "It's now or never, take two or three bundles, you can throw out the merguez and whatever else you don't want!"

I bought three bundles and compared with the woman from Guadeloupe; once I sorted through mine I came away with just a kilo of entrecôte! The rest was too greasy for a pot-au-feu or too bony for a ragout. I left what I didn't want in the pile of scraps near the street, because those without the money even for the bundles were already beginning to appear in the market to rifle through what others had thrown out. My parcel was gathered quickly and I didn't feel like I had thrown away my money! Even so! . . .

June 11, 1963

My husband is back from Paris. He went to some ministries, he came back without a job, but he's happy he "made the trip," he saw some kind of department head and an orderly who knows everything. Fortunately, Carolina, there is that type of person. They give courage to those who hope to air their problems to a minister who is absolutely inaccessible to the poor bastards here on earth. I played along half-heartedly, he noticed and said to me, tongue-in-cheek:

"I went to see your journalist! I had to open the letter to remind myself of his name. One thing is for certain: He's not writing small town news, he has an office and an assistant at the front, I tried to see him twice in the same day, no use, he comes and goes as he pleases with no set hours. Don't expect a response . . . When he sees that opened letter! . . . Imagine the look on his face! The assistant took it from me anyway and told me to come back."

"But he'll read my letter, the assistant said?"

"At this point . . . Who cares whether he reads it or not! I had to catch my train home, I didn't have time to go back. You didn't think I was going to lose another day of work for this nonsense."

And so the case is closed. In any event, I'm happy to know this journalist hasn't died, and I have bigger fish to fry.

June 12, 1963

Cécile has come back from her honeymoon; with the summer and her newfound happiness, she is radiant. This winter, they'll wait for nicer days side by side. Cécile strongly advised me to go to Paris myself! The city is teeming with editors. She also reminded me that it wasn't a joke when the literary agent wrote "Maméga, woman of letters." Then I showed her the quote he offered to have my manuscript corrected, and that was no joke either. And so this is "The End" of my scribbling, and for now I'll settle for dreaming that it will be a real book one day.

June 15, 1963

I'm going to cover for Renée while she has her appendix taken out. She's been having stomach pain for three months now, but she's so afraid of her lady that she would still be at her job if I hadn't told her that she was risking a major crisis. I asked her, Carolina, if her employers were aware of her pain. She answered that her lady kept saying that she hadn't paid for Renée's trip from the West Indies to Marseille just for her to get sick. She added: "Madame said that I can have my operation once I've finished reimbursing her the 90,000 francs she loaned me for the trip."

All of that happened in a gathering of haughty "elite" negroes who didn't want to hear any talk of problems with West Indian "domestics." However, Carolina, since Bécassine no longer comes down from Brittany, Doudou took over; she is found in the most unexpected areas of France.* Let me tell

*Bécassine is a white housemaid character from a French comic strip. The implication here is that because provincial white French women no longer come into the cities to be housekeepers, now Doudou (Créole/Caribbean women) have taken over their work.—Tr.

you, I have a foolish spinster cousin who ended up working for a family on the Pyrenees border, and it's no walk in the park for her. When she goes to the village, all the kids follow her, real savages, she tells me! I can't talk about any of that when we're among other West Indians. Renée pretends that she's an executive secretary in front of the elite. But she can't pull one over on me! I looked at her calloused hands and said: "So, how's it going in your lady's house?" She seemed embarrassed and she finally came clean when I made it clear that I didn't show off all the time around a punch bowl with the town big shots.

Gradually, I understood that she was in hot water up to her neck and that she wasn't trying to get out of it, bound by a deep fear of her white employers.

Since her life might well depend on it, I offered to replace her for two weeks: otherwise, she would have kept her infected appendix for another eight months, the time it'll take to work off her debt.

June 16, 1963

I set off in a low neckline to Renée's bosses' house because when it's cold, I really bundle myself up, and when it's hot, I can't bear to have anything around my neck or arms.

The lady is chubby and impressively neat in appearance. For the first time since I launched myself into this profession as a cleaning woman, I have a first name; the lady gave it to me. She doesn't want to change her habits, I'm the one who will change names: I'll be called Renée until the real Renée returns. No ifs ands or buts about it. They'll call me Renée, and I'll answer when I realize they're referring to me.

June 17, 1963

One year in the profession, Carolina, and I am more and more certain that when people claim that our work doesn't impact our physique, it's magical thinking. I had turned back into a woman by staying home, and now here I am again, dripping with sweat, "dusting behind the furniture." I am transformed into an exploited machine, and not a very malleable one, because Madame almost choked when I didn't answer her call simply because my name is not Renée. She said to me: "Renée is nicer than you! I hope her illness doesn't last long!" I really got on her last nerve when I told her that I was making arrangements for the aforementioned Renée to go to a nursing home. That earned me a punishment and I had to push a rag around in the most unthinkable parts of the place. These are the first days, I'm having a whale of a time, but she's also getting on my last nerve; she'll need to find herself another Renée.

I finished my four hours of cleaning in such a state that I looked like one of the old things piled up in the attic where I spent my last hour of work. I brushed my hair with my hands, I smoothed my skirt in the hallway before walking onto the street, and I went to see Renée. The real one.

Madame, who doesn't take the bus, arrived at the clinic before me. Renée seemed horrified to see me. The lady then stood up and said to Renée: "See you soon! As we agreed, right, Renée?"

Renée murmured something back.

She waited five whole minutes before speaking to me, out of fear that her lady might come back and listen to our conversation. Finally, she burst out:

"I can't go to the nursing home, the lady said so! You don't stay at her house long enough! Four hours is too little for her! I would get up at seven in the morning and go to sleep at midnight sometimes."

"No wonder it's not just your intestines that are infected! Your doctor said that you have a serious case of anemia and that you need to increase your red blood cell count; by winter you'll be completely shattered from those fifteen or sixteen hours of work per day!"

I was exasperated because I could tell that she was going to refuse to take time off. An invisible thread was holding her back.

She repeated: "I haven't paid her back yet! I haven't paid her back yet!"

She was too tired tonight; I left without resolving the issue.

June 19, 1963

I greeted the family with a resounding: "Bonjour messieurs-dames!"

The girls continued to do their hair in the vestibule with their backs to me, and Madame began: "Renée! You'll have to work quickly! There's the ironing and the windows to do!"

A ladder was already leaning against the wall. In this ancient Prado house, the windows were higher than church doors. From the six-story windows, people and things below look like miniatures. I told myself that I had to keep my composure so as not to topple into the void when I'm at the top of the ladder. Imperturbable, Madame continued: "Your friend couldn't lift her arms to scrub the windows: it hasn't been done for the last two months! You, at least, don't have a stomachache!"

It wasn't a stomachache I had, but a heartache.

So she was aware of the serious pain of the little Martiniquan who had washed up at her door! And she kept her here, inhumanely, for the sake of money!

Carolina, it makes me even sicker than Renée when I think about it.

I ironed a mountain of laundry, my thoughts elsewhere. I cleaned the bay windows with no desire to laugh, I was too focused to worry about anything happening below, I ignored my vertigo and set one foot on the ladder and the other on the edge of the window to clean the outside pane. I tried to picture myself standing firmly on the ground, in a cellar perhaps. Monsieur came out, his towel under his arm. His voice wrested me from my reverie.

He yelled: "Get down from there! Come on, get down!"

He hurried into the living room, mopping his brow. I heard him unleash his anger in a harried voice: "Have you gone mad! I told you to call a specialized company to clean the window panes! From the street, I saw people looking up here, I followed their gaze and saw the woman scrubbing those damn windows! If she wants to kill herself, let her do it somewhere else!"

I came down, their squabble left me indifferent. I was still picturing the girl unable to lift her arms because her stomach hurt too badly.

The lady brought me back to reality: "Fine: clean the birdcage and leave!"

If one has the power to say "Do it! Get going! Go up! Come down!" it should always be said kindly.

June 25, 1963

I'm too tired to write to you, my dear Carolina, and too discouraged. Renée decided not to take time off because she wants to buy her emancipation as soon as possible.

Such is life, and I regret not being African because African women aren't cleaning ladies. The French don't bring women over from that continent; they are subconsciously too enamored with freedom.

June 30, 1963

Renée has returned to the house. Monsieur was in a good mood when they got back from the clinic, and Renée has lost a lot of weight. Monsieur knows the Canary Islands, he told me that in such countries people die young because there are no seasons. He asked me the average mortality of West Indian people, and I remarked that he knows a lot about the Third World. So if Renée croaks, it's because of her natural lifespan as an inhabitant of the Third World, it can't be helped. It's a point of view that Renée will easily internalize, with all the resignation she has in her.

June 30, 1963

My little old lady sent me a long letter. She could have been happy in her sun-filled nursing home, but she's nostalgic for her house, filled with memories. My dear Carolina, I was so surprised to receive a letter from my old Provençale that I had to reread it two more times to convince myself that there are still people somewhere who can love someone or something other than themselves.

Chapter Twelve

July 3, 1963

Solange has now moved, she bought a small apartment and is setting out to go punch holes in metro tickets. She added, laughing, that she was "moving on up." I wonder if Solange will get used to living underground. She invited me to toast her next chapter at a negro ball sponsored by officials from Paris.

Before leaving, I had to put my kids to bed and wait for the student who was supposed to watch them. She showed up exhausted and sprawled on my little girl's corner seat. I was overcome with immense pity because she told me that many nights she can't go to bed until she puts down babies who want nothing more than to stay awake, and then the next day she takes a very early bus to the university in Aix. I told her: "Take a load off tonight and get some sleep! The kids aren't babies anymore." She didn't need to be told twice, and by the time the three of us left she was sound asleep.

Solange is bubbly as usual, she speaks of the future with confidence, she claims to have learned how to live by observing her employers: "As domestic servants, we are inoculated against any ideas about the future, because that's how we most comfortably shed any claim to human dignity; we are a thing, like a broom or a refrigerator! Even if I become rich one day, I'm disgusted by the idea of hiring a maid, for fear of becoming like those women who somehow claim to be Christians! What a joke!"

A hundred mixed couples were listening to a European talk about the West Indies. They seated us near a band of youths determined to enjoy themselves no matter the cost and impatiently awaiting the end of this clichéd speech. The young people managed to attract the attention of a portion of the audience by sketching portraits on scraps of paper. The drawings were comical and people laughed. The officials, in response to this unexpected commotion, tried to look away as officially as possible.

Lunch was served: there was a mad dash for the buffets. I asked Father Something how he could eat so much charcuterie; it's wild how hungry people get when there's a free lunch! You'd think they never eat at home! I saw a friend of my employers who loves oysters. She looked at me with visible astonishment. She said: "Where have I seen you before?"

I answered: "On a train in blue coveralls!"

It's wild how clothes make the man around here!

All the girls who work as maids on rue Paradis or in Saint-Giniez were there: they had heard about this West Indian soirée on the radio. Each one was more elegant than the last. They must have worked quite a lot of hours to be able to afford such pretty dresses. They had also been pestered by the women of the house to finish the dishes before getting dressed. More than one, in the middle of painting her nails, must have heard "her lady" say: "Shine my shoes for tomorrow!"

And yet they arrived fresh and smiling, though slightly timid. They managed to find a spot for themselves, because the elite folks ignored them completely. For the elites, who bragged about being close friends with the most high-profile personalities, these girls were an eyesore. They felt a need to display a certain stiffness, for fear of hearing a girl announce: "That's my cousin!"

More and more young maids arrived, and, my dear Carolina, I was happy to finally see them outside the context of their daily yoke. Perhaps they could become human once again like everyone else in this moment . . . I spoke too soon: one of the elites approached a group of pretty girls who were paying their share and said: "Who invited you? This ball isn't for you! There are VIPs here."

One of them replied: "This is a West Indian ball, is it not? When I go to a Corsican ball, I receive a much better welcome!"

I called to a server who was passing by: "Those girls over there, find them a seat, they paid, don't just leave them standing there! The officials pay nothing and they're seated with their wives, the friends of their friends, so go on!"

The server, flustered, went to find chairs, but said to me: "I'm not the one leaving them standing there! The Black man in charge gives the orders, I just execute them! But why doesn't he want those girls here?"

While he was speaking, a girl with doe eyes dressed in sky blue, accompanied by a timid boy, came to my table in tears. "The Martiniquan in the white jacket who is the leader of your club insulted me, he said to me again and again: "Do you belong here?" Well, where do I belong then? Not at my lady's house! I am and will always be the foreigner, because of my skin, and here, among the negroes, they tell me I don't belong either, because I'm a maid! If I go to rue Thubaneau, maybe I'll be treated better!"

There was a lot of bitterness in her words. We embraced, and Solange called: "Garçon, champagne for everyone! Just let that guy try to stop you! Then even the officials will know that he's a vile racist negro! And that's the guy who's supposed to lead us!"

The boy who was with the girl in blue took her by the arms: "Come on! Let's go to the Catalans! They don't cause problems for us in that neighborhood, at least we can still dance in the European balls! We'll go get our money back!"

And he dragged his partner away.

The girl who was told to "leave," shunted about everywhere like a wisp of straw, shook my hand and disappeared into the night, taking her disillusionment with her, and mine. But why are there negroes who draw the curtain over our negritude? We don't heal a wound by hiding it, quite the opposite.

A few pranksters heard about it and showed up, determined to cause mayhem: "So this is how it is, there's a West Indian event and you turn away West Indians who slave away, while we're the largest population in Marseille to work on the quays and on rue Paradis! There aren't any West Indian supervisors! So what do you mean, 'No maids,' when the girls can't do anything else? If they were on rue Thubaneau, we could understand why the elites blush! But those poor girls work honestly, stashed in houses by the same people who turn them away today!"

The young man at the register was afraid that the officials would catch wind of what was going on, so he let them in; they puffed out their chests, a server bowed to them and an elite flashed them a warm smile. Carolina, that's the way of the world, might makes right, and I thought of the girl with nails eaten away by cleaning products, with no defense but her tears.

Solange, in her imagistic language, told me that in Paris, there is an office called the BUMIDOM which is responsible for workers from overseas territories.

"It would be great if this service had social workers who could discreetly look into the lives of girls who end up as maids in these places! Some of them are minors! But the protection of minors doesn't apply to West Indians: we are born minor!"

She laughed, but her laugh had a tragic air to it.

July 4, 1963

This is my last job before summer vacation: my baker asked me to find her a seamstress for a mom who lives in a neighboring area. When I told her that I could do it, she seemed skeptical. It's because I strut around in my little adopted village, and my baker imagines that I'm a mom with no money problems; when I'm too broke, I go to the pawnshop, she has no idea that some days I count my coins to buy the daily bread. Once I have the bread, I forget that I counted coins, or that I had to give up a piece of jewelry that will lie dormant in the pawnshop waiting for me to come back for it.

July 6, 1963

The little Corsican girl has five boys, as unruly as mine, a little less polite, but there is almost perfect harmony between us. This morning they said "the negress," but tonight they call me "Mamèga." I simply said to them: "I don't call you 'the little gingers,' even though you are! I am a negress, but I have a name, you know!"

Their mom, surprised, listened to me and said to them: "The lady is right, it's not very nice." She gave me a basket of blue jeans to cut and turn into shorts, a pile of socks to sort through; she set up a sewing machine in a corner of the kitchen and told me to begin.

I hadn't cut even two pairs of shorts before she asked me to help her hang laundry on the lines suspended from the courtyard's fruit trees; then, I peeled the vegetables and helped her to make the seven beds. Tonight, I put the two unfinished pairs of shorts back in the work basket. At this rate, the sewing won't be finished for a while.

July 8, 1963

I polished the villa stairs, I painted the rungs of the gate, I shined the chairs and washed the kids' bicycles sitting in the garage. Sewing is now out of the question: the work basket has disappeared.

July 9, 1963

Voilà: it's summer vacation, and I still have five days to go. Madame is kind, she speaks of her country and tells me she is amazed that I was able to win her children's respect in so little time. Perhaps I could stay at her house, she says. Sewing is out of the question.

July 11, 1963

A young girl came to sew the shorts. Finally I said to Madame: "I thought you hired me for the sewing!"

I feigned naiveté. Madame answered me: "I've wanted a Black cleaning woman for so long! When you showed up, I didn't dare tell you right away, but you fit the bill! Can't you stay longer? I'm not going on vacation until August!"

I had come as a seamstress and, without asking my opinion, she had kindly handed me her brooms, it was only natural. I could have walked away from day one, but I had wanted to see how long and how far this would go! And now I know! My dear Carolina, I feel no bitterness, because this is how it is. We are categorized by the government and all of France as cleaning women above all, just as the Poles are agricultural workers or the Algerians road workers. It's a pervasive notion that keeps gaining traction, and Madame, who is not at all cruel, simply puts into practice what she's heard. Voilà: it's unthinkable for a typist not to be a typist, for a seamstress not to be a seamstress off the bat. I didn't explain this to Madame, she wouldn't have understood. I just said that my ten days of sewing would come to an end in five days, and that I would take care of my own kids over summer vacation. My insistent repetition of the words mending and sewing embarrassed her and she didn't insist.

July 13, 1963

It's my last afternoon at the little Corsican's house, I didn't mend a single pair of socks.

Seven o'clock. It's still light out, and Madame takes advantage of my labor down to the last second: from the cellar to the attic, we tackled everything, my face was gray with dust, I hid my fatigue because once I'm gone, when Madame has an Italian or Marseillaise woman, I want her to realize that she took things too far, and for her to say in good faith: "I really did go too far with the Black woman." I pushed the big oil-fired stove into the cellar, I carried the wool throws to the attic in wicker baskets, I filled a crack the kids made in the garage with putty, I washed the large stone staircase three times while the kids went up and down without waiting for it to dry, I unclogged the pipe that connects the water tank to the villa. Madame said in her sweet little voice: "Do this for me since you're not coming back!" She didn't add: "Since no white woman would do it." I granted her the pleasure of possessing a Black woman to the last minute, and I left laughing down the path that takes me home.

July 14, 1963

Last night, I put a thick layer of cream on my face, I need to look like a new woman, I'm leaving soon for Allauch with a few girls from my country to dance the beguine.

On the bus to the bustling town, the driver told me that I had to pay for two seats to accommodate my skirt, and he added mischievously: "Hey, I'd be happy to hold that thing for you!" So much good humor made me forget the week's absurd chores. There's one thing that can't be camouflaged: a person's hands are like their business card. Today mine have almost no nails, and they're all wrinkled despite the coat of glycerin I applied. So I put on my gloves. Since I joined the hellish world of domestic workers, my forehead reveals my anxiety, and I have to make an effort to seem nonchalant. The two little maids with me similarly have trouble finding the confidence displayed by the other girls who have a home of their own.

Oh well! Provence calls! Time to forget our troubles. I dressed my daughter in her best outfit, and all around me people from town applaud as she walks by.

On the main square, amidst the smell of crêpes and pizza, a green pagan divinity, part dragon, part crocodile, and part lion, presided over the festivities on an antique wooden chariot. I thought I was dreaming, that I had been transported to Africa. I asked a young girl who was devoutly touching the thing's paws what it was, she told me that it was the Allauch town emblem, which is brought out only once per year. I had to settle for this explanation, altogether plausible. My companions passed from one stall to another as onlookers watched indulgently. Night fell, warm and gray, adding to the atmosphere. The men dressed as Nordic devils were determined to enjoy themselves as much as possible. They clicked their boots and jingled their bells and, among the plane trees, their white plumes stood out starkly between the lowest branches. A prancing devil circled around my attractive compatriot. He was likely the leader of that jingling bunch. They had more plumes than a field of blooming sugarcane. That forest leaned forward, backward, right, left, as if moved by an invisible breath. It couldn't have been the mistral, because the weather was completely calm. The jolly fellow stared at Suzette more and more insistently, he wiped his forehead, spat, gave orders to his followers who were resting or prancing about, and he went back to Suzette, proud of his conquest. She played along with his little game by throwing him cheeky winks: it worked on the leader, who forgot about his companions.

He approached our group and said to Suzette: "Why do you lift your dress like that? You're riling me up!" The very pretty girl started to laugh and the devil approached her intrepidly, he was completely flushed. His friends followed suit and mixed into our group, singing. I didn't want to be inundated by these demons. The one who grabbed my waist didn't speak French well and whistled in surprise, I was certainly not as pretty as the young girls I was with, and I had a stern gaze. I sent him off to go make a racket somewhere else: "It's a parade, not a mixer! With your headdresses, you'll block us from view!"

He wasn't frightened, because, under the cloak of an opportune shadow, he angled his big red face towards mine!

Suzette couldn't stop laughing: "Look, even Maméga has found herself a Nordic man tonight!"

I pushed him away and retorted that it was her fault we had all these devils at our heels, that she had to stop provoking these fellows: "Real devils! They're not just wearing costumes!"

Meanwhile, in luminous Allauch, the regional groups filed through to the cheers of the crowd gathered along the main road.

I turned back toward the head devil and yelled: "For God's sake! We're crossing through the city, get ahold of yourself!"

He emitted some guttural noises at the devils lost in our ranks.

Suzette deployed her skirt and readjusted her madras,

she clicked her high heels while the crowd applauded wildly. Suddenly, I heard my name: it was the little Corsican woman and her bunch, they had seen me and couldn't contain themselves, the kids were hot on my heels. I turned to my most recent lady, her eyes were wide: "You didn't tell me that you participated in these things! I thought you would be resting today!"

I believed it, and she was right to think so: anyone other than me would have been completely exhausted after being at her house, and it was precisely to ascribe that fatigue to something else that I was out tonight.

I answered almost cheerfully: "One doesn't say such things to their employers!"

She looked at my hands in their nylon gloves, those hands that had been covered in grease, paint, and corrosives twenty-four hours ago, she looked at my hairdo which the girls had done for me, she looked at my high heels, she who had only ever seen my slippers and my hair wrapped in a scarf, she didn't understand, it was as if I had played a dirty trick on her. Utterly relaxed, I bought ice cream for her kids who were feasting their eyes on my little girl with her collier-choux. And then poof! I disappeared into the ranks, relegating them forevermore to my memories, one of the least disagreeable of my life as a cleaning lady, because Madame merely applied the theory "hard labor for the Black woman." And I had slaved away without ever imagining that Madame could have thought any differently.

When the parade was over, my plumed devil approached me and asked for a souvenir. I gave him a little silk scarf on behalf of my group, which he stuffed into a pocket of his puffy blouse.

Suzette couldn't stop laughing: "Imagine me showing up in the West Indies with my blond devil! What would my mother say?"

"You should really be thinking about what his mother would say if you fell madly in love with him!" I answered.

That was like a cold shower for her and she calmed down.

The two maids tried to act like everyone else, but in vain; they are marked by servitude. I can easily shake off the moral yoke involved in this damned profession because I have my own home, my own family. But I have so much sympathy for these girls, bound day and night to serving those damn ladies.

Later that night, I put away my finery with a sigh of relief. An obligatory two-month break is very welcome; I'll be able to make good on my plan and take a trip up to Paris.

Chapter Thirteen

July 16, 1963

No kids leaving for school, no lady to dust for, a tropical sun, a few francs in my purse: euphoria! And, the cherry on top, I don't have to get up at six in the morning. I found my slippers and an old robe that I must never have worn. Yesterday I made jars of jam "for winter," which the children have already started dipping into. And that mountain of mending I've accumulated! There is in fact a lot to do in my home, I could use a cleaning lady of my own.

July 18, 1963

Solange wrote to me from Paris, she is delighted with her new life. Of course, winter is still far away. She tells me to hurry up and come if I want to find a publishing house that's still open. I decided not to worry about the literary agent who asked me for too much money. Perhaps by going to see Gallimard or Julliard, I won't have bills to pay immediately, and I am determined to figure it out on my own. Solange tells me to come, but she adds: "I did some research, it will be an uphill battle; you have no connections, no name of any consequence, you are nothing, and they do nothing for those who are nothing, unless you have a lot of money to spend; my nephew at university told me this, he said to convince you to scrap it all; in any case you can come, it's beautiful and your children will see the Eiffel Tower."

Better to be forewarned, that way I won't be disappointed. I'll go see for myself, Carolina. Resignation is not always a bad thing.

July 20, 1963

I'm always happy to remove my robe at six o'clock when the cicadas are already chanting. There are shrubs all around my house and the midsummer enchantment automatically relaxes my every gesture.

I have started to pack the suitcases because we're all leaving for Paname next week, except for Papa.*

Madame Roland came over tonight while I was folding the last pair of kids' crew socks. It seems like nothing, a half-dozen pairs of the things to mend, and yet my afternoon flew by. Madame Roland saw how busy I was and asked why I seemed to be in such a rush. And then she said: "My daughter doesn't have time off until August 6, she works in a lawyer's office; her coworker already left, so she's the only one taking care of things, and what do you know, in the middle of summer, she has a sore throat. I thought you could take her place until the sixth, you know how it is; if a white woman takes over for her, she might not be able to get her job back. I don't want my little girl to end up cleaning houses

*Panāme is a slang term for Paris.—Tr.

like me; I slaved away for so many years to send her to technical school, she graduated from Marie Curie, you know, the big school near Boulevard Chave. Even so she faced some unspeakable difficulties finding herself a job."

I answered: "I'm leaving on vacation, I'm going to Paris with the little ones for ten days: I'm leaving the twenty-fifth and I come back August 11, it's already settled."

Madame Roland started to cry, and that made my arms go limp and my guts churn.

"It's not that the lawyer couldn't find a replacement, quite the contrary! But I don't want her to lose her position. I told her to say that she's sending someone for ten days, I thought you could do it, since you're on vacation!"

Exactly, I'm on vacation, and I don't want to see the ladies and gentlemen in their offices or in their homes, I've had enough of that. But the woman was crying, she trusted me, she thought that I could perform a less degrading profession. She hadn't looked at my nailless hands; I had managed to lighten them, but they bear no resemblance to a secretary's hands. In a pinch, when I'm not wrapped in blue coveralls, my clothing could be suitable, but nothing would fix my ruined fingers. Rheumatism already afflicts my deformed knuckles each time I dip them in the ice-cold basins at the ladies' homes, and it makes me terribly self-conscious.

I said to Madame Roland: "You see! My hands are all stiff and I've lost all the agility I need for this profession! And then there's my trip: how am I supposed to push it back by ten days?"

You don't just tell everyone that you're going to find an editor in Paris with hands like these, for fear that the entire city will have a laugh about it. Vacation is an excellent alibi. My husband had arrived in the meantime. He heard about Madame Roland's request and my hesitation and he shouted: "For once you have a chance to drop the pots and pans and try something else, but you're so caught up in your documentation! You will be so saturated with this life that you'll never be able to get out of it!"

That horrified me: the idea of not being able to get out of servitude for the rest of my life, it was unthinkable! I can still picture Aunt Jeanne all crippled in the Parisian suburbs, after spending thirty years of her life in others' homes. She has social security and the old-age pension, but not an ounce of gratitude from those that she watched come into the world, grow up, get married. And yet, she loved that family more than her own relatives! Now she has nothing left but memories, a brown ringlet from the little bourgeois girl she saw go through life, a plaster dog that they gave her one New Year's Day, and resignation. When I see her, she always speaks to me about her employers, without bitterness, with pride:

"Thirty years I stayed with them! Those were the days! There was the war that shook up our way of life, the young people don't remember it anymore and the old people were so worried!"

I admire her so much that I don't dare tell her that I don't want to end up like her. I understand her, but my soul is appalled.

I had slipped away, I wasn't with Madame Roland anymore, I was thinking of Aunt Jeanne. The intrepid lady noticed:

"So, is that a yes?"

"Yes!"

My husband let out an oof of relief: "Maybe going to the office again will detoxify you."

When August knocks on the door, nothing detoxifies except for open air and freedom. I said yes anyway and Madame Roland left reassured. Tonight, I am neither content nor angry. I rub cream on my stiff fingers to properly face the keys of my typewriter.

July 20, 1963

I returned to the office feeling confident, determined not to tell anyone that I clean other people's homes. I quickly lost my haughtiness, because the lawyer had already seen me at the doctor's house, on a day when he had come with his wife for tea. My ears turned red and I waited for him to tell me to go clean the landing. There was an initial moment of surprise that passed quickly, and he said to me with kindness: "So, you know how to do everything? Good, go get yourself set up in that office!"

I had prepared myself for everything except that; I stammered: "It's only for a few days, the girl will be better soon!"

I wanted to cry, and I realized that my time in the aroma of others' lives had marked me, made me self-conscious.

I took refuge behind the mobile table where a pile of folders awaited me pitilessly. The lawyer said to me: "Answer the clients, use the standard formulas, I wrote down the most important, refer to the folders!"

Fortunately he left, the dear master! Everything seemed incomprehensible to me: I reread the first letter five times in a row. With each telephone call, I dropped my text and feverishly picked up the headset. "Hello! No, Maître isn't here! Please leave a message."

I didn't dare say at any point: "Secretary speaking!" as I should have. My interlocutors were invisible, and yet I thought I could see their scrutinizing eyes asking where they had seen me before, in which houses, in the homes of which ladies. Since I've started amusing myself by changing employers as often as I change stockings, I have to be prepared for surprises. Voilà, Carolina, the day is over, my embarrassment too. It's so hot that I don't want to go to bed, I type, I type, but to write to you, and suddenly I feel my hands relax, I'm in familiar territory, confidence always makes miracles. Maître Bracci was far superior to my typical bosses. He patiently corrected my spelling errors and told me that I had a very nice style. That was enough for me to forget at the end of the day that he had once seen me dusting a desk rather than sitting behind one.

July 24, 1963

I take two buses to Maître Bracci's office, I arrive in a daze, I rush to the narrow room that has just one window overlooking the courtyard, I see the red roofs blocking the horizon and imprisoning the rays of the Saharan sun. I dream of a hammock, and Maître, impeccably dressed, looks like something out of a Canebière store window. After two pages of typing I start to sweat, there's no breeze and the fan doesn't work, I wipe my forehead incessantly, Maître gently loosens his tie and says: "What will become of us if it keeps on like this? Lucky for you, you're used to this heat!" He really said that! If I was used to being hot without being able to open the door or shutters or without walking barefoot on a waxed parquet floor, I've surely forgotten. I suffer terribly from the heat, all the more so since I've become Europeanized; I walk in full sun with no parasol and no pandan sunhat, even when the solar equator peaks over Marseille.

I type, type, and type again. I take or sort sheets of paper in a crowd of multicolored and meticulously ironed shirts. I can answer without stammering now. I suffocate from heat despite opening my blouse as much as possible. Maître is usually away from his practice. Once he leaves, my fingers work while my spirit roams: half-priced SNCF tickets, I'll go to Paris, I'll see Paris again, I'll go to the department stores! I'll walk the Champs-Élysées with the kids. Meanwhile, work happens and six o'clock arrives; in the waiting room, the clients wipe their brows too as they wait for the boss to arrive.

He enters, already beginning the conversation, taking notes, seemingly impervious to the heat. He signs the mail that I place in an envelope before slipping it into the nearest mailbox. And I arrive back home completely out of breath and immediately jump into a rejuvenating shower.

July 27, 1963

When I lower my eyes to avoid seeing those steaming keys bathed in sharp clarity, my gaze plunges toward the building across the way, to a floor where a woman's voice drones on every afternoon. It intrigues me, I hear it but can't see it. It was horrendously hot the other afternoon and the heat wave enabled me to see who possessed such a commanding voice. A large woman opened the shutters that had been concealing a noisy and strange gathering.

The woman invoked the grace and strength of God and yelled: "Silence, please!" Then she called the names of a list of people; I understood that she directed a Jewish charity group. She said, vigorously, bitterly: "Take your seats! It's not your day! I already saw you yesterday! I can't help you!"

With the window open, her voice overcame the sound of my keyboard and I stopped typing so I could understand what was happening. I heard: "I can't help you," and saw an old woman in mourning all hunched over staring in a daze at the large woman directing the charity. Maître left and I had finished my mail: leisurely I watched the old woman come back several times to ask for the assistance of the person who had cavalierly prayed to a charitable God a few moments ago. The large woman was losing her patience now with the old desperate beggar: "I don't want to hear it! I can't help you!" That made my blood run cold and my hair stand on end. We can always do something for someone. A comforting word, a polite refusal, a sympathetic look. What's the use in serving in the name of God if our heart is empty? I was saddened by that thought, and I didn't notice that Maître Bracci had entered, he saw that I was staring opposite and simply said: "It's sad here! Only the people across the way provide a change of scenery, you're right to let yourself unwind!" I couldn't believe it! In eighteen months no one has ever said that to me, quite the opposite!

Carolina, I have to revise my perspective, but first I'd like to know whether Maître would treat me the same way if I were pushing a broom around his home!

Now, to write to you, Carolina, I have a system: I wedge my notebook into my handbag for the bus ride, along with a Bic pen. My commute takes nearly an hour and I utilize this wasted time as best I can: I write nonstop. This intrigued the woman in gray who is always sitting on the seat opposite mine. She asked me whom I was writing to, I answered without pausing:

"To Carolina!"

"Is that your daughter?"

"No, she's my sister!"

She didn't seem convinced, muttering: "I bet you're writing to your lover!"

She's delusional, nowadays people don't write to their lovers, they call to set up meetings. I thought that and smiled; the woman in gray felt validated in her thoughts: "Ah yes, I guessed it," she said.

That woman has definitively wiped from my memory the large woman who says no.

July 29, 1963

Madame Roland comes to feed my children, because I don't have time to breathe and at the office you can't show up late like at the ladies' houses. And I have to keep up this rhythm all day: back home at night, I see heads barely defrizzed, sandals without laces. Madame Roland can't impose discipline on this bunch that thinks only of chasing cicadas until we can go to Paris. Today, Maître served me a refreshment. How far away last summer seems, when, to soothe my throat catching fire under the fluorescent lights of a lady's home, I had no recourse other than to run my tongue over my dry lips. I can attest to the fact that jobs are ridiculous; depending on whether you're a cleaning woman or a woman of letters, your status switches from beast of burden to human being. And yet, my dear Carolina, my fingers are still completely stiff and I am the same; so cry, cry my soul, for there are many more of my sisters in the first category than in the second. When will the chains they didn't forge be broken for good! I drank the beverage, and Maître saw my troubled expression. He said: "You can open the window, really, this heatwave is crushing everyone." Voilà: it's almost over. The girl will come back to her office and I will head up to Paris, just in time, I think, to find all the publishing houses closed. It will do me a world of good as I await the return to school and the future bullfights in ladies' homes.

August 2, 1963

Maître Bracci paid me royally, I rushed straight to the station to buy our tickets. I sent a telegram to Solange telling her to meet us at Gare de Lyon. The children are bubbling over with excitement. Paris for the first time, it's a marvelous world for them.

August 4, 1963

After stuffing my pages and my hopes for finding an editor into a briefcase, it was time to cram my children, wild with joy, into a taxi. My husband will have to cook for himself. Solange will meet us right on time.

Chapter Fourteen

August 5, 1963

This morning I found Paris exactly as I left it ten years ago: silent, humid, and orderly. The half-asleep children blended into the crowd of travelers waiting in line for a taxi. My little girl, who is a true Marseillaise, asked me why the police officer directing the long line wasn't speaking. In Marseille, all the police officers speak. Fortunately, Solange is still a Provençale; she told us stories in a deafening voice, the process to get herself hired as a cleaning woman in a hospital, her adventures in the employment offices. Finally, I put together that she was an usher in her neighborhood cinema: "It's an easy job, I say 'Follow me, monsieur,' 'This way, madame,' no one notices that I don't speak French very well." She said that with a laugh, and the silent and tired crowd stared at her incredulously. My littlest one cried:

"Maman, why are the people in Paris sad? Why is it like this?"

"They're not sad, in Paris this is how you're supposed to be, even in summer, everyone is in a rush and it makes them gloomy."

Solange laughed: "Even the taxi drivers are like that, almost to the point of rudeness. You realize, with this beautiful summer, in Marseille, the driver would have suggested that we go for a swim in Plages des Catalans; he would have said it just to make conversation, but he would have said it, while this one, he's deaf and almost blind."

The driver Solange was speaking about had placed our luggage in the trunk of his car, and suddenly he realized that there were seven of us. "I can't take all of you, figure it out, I have things to do."

It was decided. Solange and three kids would cram into the taxi with the unfriendly driver, and I would go in another car being mobbed by antsy travelers. She said to the driver: "We're going to Villejuif." I repeated the same thing to my cabby, recommending that we follow the first car. Without a glance, without a word, he took off.

Jean-Pierre continued: "Why is he sad, the monsieur, why is he like that?"

After Porte d'Italie, without a hitch, we arrived at the little street where Solange lives. She pushed open the wooden gate and entered the small detached house that was tiny, tiny, like an attic.

"Here we are," she said, "this is my place! I'm going to enlarge it bit by bit. To pay for it, I sold my jewelry and even my 2CV, I poured my savings from the last twenty years into this. My husband is happy; when he arrives in Le Havre, he'll be able to come here or I can go there! Speaking of Le Havre, good grief! You should see how many negroes wash up there, many more than in Cannes or Marseille! I went to see my husband, the quays were full of West Indians, I thought I was in Fort-de-France! What's going on over there to make all the inhabitants of the island pack up and leave?"

While she was speaking, she lost no time: in less than

fifteen minutes, she had turned her minuscule living room into a bedroom. She had placed crisp white sheets on the two divans, transforming them into beds. She was astonishing, deafening: "I've kept the habit of doing everything in a rush, I still feel as though there's a lady at my heels! My husband asks me what's wrong with me, always jumping out of bed. I've been scarred, and I can't figure out how to live leisurely. I'm on break, or rather I asked for forty-eight hours off, we'll go to the flea market in Bicêtre!"

I opened the curtains, I saw a small plot of dirt with a dozen lettuce plants in front of the small cottage that Solange called "mon pavillon." She was so proud of her tidy nest that I went along with it, and I hoped that she would soon achieve her dream of expanding it.

August 6, 1963

Two days in Paris with Solange is an incredible thing. She brought me to Les Halles bright and early while my children were still asleep, I met all the West Indians walking between the crates of vegetables or the cases of fish. They spoke Creole, they shouted to each other: it wasn't sad, this morning, in that gray market. We bought a bonito for seven francs and two large baskets of vegetables for next to nothing. We let ourselves be tempted by the modest prices without thinking about how we would bring all these things back on the metro. By the time we got to Porte d'Italie, we were exhausted: we signaled for a taxi. Once we got the kids ready to go, it was already noon.

I told Solange that if things continued like this, the Marseillais wouldn't have time to see Paris. She knew what to do, she went to find a car for the day at a nearby garage and she crammed us into the Aronde, informing us that she knew Paris well. "In case of an accident," she added, "no need to worry, because all the traffic cops are West Indian." She said this with a laugh. Astonished, I realized that Solange wasn't kidding, she knew her way around perfectly well. She headed for the quays and presented them to us with fairly decent commentary.

At Quai Branly, the children started to jump for joy, shouting: "It's so beautiful now! Paris is sad at five in the morning, but in the middle of the afternoon, in summer, when the quays belong to you, it's like paradise!" Solange brusquely slammed the brakes of the car near a bed of tall green shrubs, the children tumbled out and ran to the foot of the Eiffel Tower. They spent all their pocket money on postcards. I had to pay for souvenir pins and miniature towers. After climbing to the second story, we were so hot that Solange shouted: "Christ! This sun is unbearable!" Of course they left amazed; after a tour of Palais de Chaillot, they decided to move to Paris since it was so pretty.

Solange told me that she had already explored all of Saint-Sulpice and noted that from there to Saint-Germain-des-Près passing through Odéon, all the publishing houses were closed.

"Don't get worked up about it! You'll go on your own in the morning to make another round while I watch the little ones, I start my job at one in the afternoon. When you're famous, remember that I was your door-to-door salesman."

My dear Carolina, better to take life as a ray of sunshine: no disappointment, no sorrow, nothing tarnishes Solange's wonderful character, and the children were delighted to have such a friend.

August 9, 1963

I got off at the Odéon metro stop, clutching an address that I had been given three months ago. Although I'd been warned, I still expected to find the first door I knocked on open.

Instead I read these words on a notice affixed to the aforementioned door: "Closed for the month of August." I jumped on a bus to Saint-Sulpice where I hoped to retrieve my pages from the hands of the literary agent, but I saw on another locked door: "Closed in August." It was already noon and I had only been able to visit two places. That depressed me and I wanted to take the train back.

August 10, 1963

While Paris is overrun by tourists obsessed with taking loads of photographs, here I am still jumping from one metro to another, from one neighborhood to another, the concierges tell me kindly that I'll have to come back in September. Today, a concierge in Saint-Michel told me to leave my pages with her. She seemed very knowledgeable about a wide range of things; for example, she told me that sometimes it takes them six months to get around to reading a manuscript, and sometimes they're never read at all. So I could leave it with her, I was nice, she would put in a good word for me. That "deflated" me all the more because my feet were hurting terribly, Solange had advised me to wear stiletto heels to be "more presentable."

I was not presentable at all, I was hobbling around, and inklings of despair made me feel the heat even more.

So as not to succumb to discouragement, I will make the pilgrimage to Montmartre. We will all go set up camp there for the rest of the day.

Solange is back at work. When I return at noon, she runs out, and she comes back late at night, so I don't see much of her.

August 12, 1963

I put on sandals and set out on the big boulevards to look for Musée Grévin. A long orderly line was already outside, flanked with restless kids. I couldn't figure out the price of entry. "Maybe it's 50 francs like the museums in Marseille," one of my kids said to me; I started to count, because money disappears so rapidly when we're on vacation that I had already stopped buying souvenirs for my neighbors, I had also told the kids to cut back on sending postcards from every post office. Visiting Musée Grévin was a must: yet when the teller gobbled up my three 1,000-franc bills in her register, it left a bitter taste in my mouth. I told the children not to ask for a Coca-Cola or peanuts because I had left the money for snacks at the counter. That dampened their enthusiasm and they looked indifferently at Robespierre, Margaret, and the other wax figures that I had been so excited to show them. The "light and sound" show managed to impress them, but it also whet their appetite, they all got thirsty at the same time. I caved and paid for their refreshments. Believe me, Carolina, I had to force myself not to shout at them that my purse was emptying rapidly. In the metro, the children, finally satisfied, voiced their astonishment at these underground journeys. Such things didn't happen under the pine trees, they would have plenty to tell their friends who had gone to the mountains! They read station names aloud and the passengers cast bewildered looks at them.

Tonight, they received a letter from their father, so they were acting impetuously; they told Solange that the big boulevards were uglier than La Canebière and that everything was more expensive than in Marseille. They asked me when we were going back. I glanced at their father's letter. He recounted the half-day he had spent at the Catalans with another family: and so, in the middle of Paris, my Marseillais started to dream of pebbles and sand castles. But before leaving, I have to go to Saint-Germain; my sole Parisian rendezvous concerning my manuscript will take place there tomorrow.

August 13, 1963

Emotional, I introduced myself to the most charming woman in Paris. She only edits historical reviews. She doled out encouragement that seemed sincere and told me to come back in September for guaranteed meetings. I collected my brood waiting for me in the hallway with the bag of provisions, full of vittles, because we had decided to set up camp in Montmartre.

To prepare me for my jaunt through sun-soaked Paris, and above all so that I would "look presentable," Solange, who had the day off, fashioned a hairstyle for me that I examine in the few storefront windows without a steel curtain in front. Solange has sensational hair, and yet, to fit with the modern trends, she has acquired an incredible collection of wigs and fake braids. She has a symmetrical face and she's pretty, even without any artifice, but that doesn't stop her from collecting creams and flasks of beauty lotion. She acquired this obsession when she was working for an esthetician. And so this morning, at the crack of dawn, she declared her intention to make me "sexy." I was rather recalcitrant when I watched her shorten my little shift dress by a good three centimeters. She started to laugh and said: "You can't go to a business meeting looking like a granny, this stuff matters, you know!"

I didn't want to be a Yé-yé girl either and I watched warily as Solange's nimble fingers shrunk my dress. When she was done, she sat me on a chair and started on my face. She grabbed creams, pomades, who knows what, and started to transform my complexion, she grabbed her makeup brushes and made two small fish of my eyes. Then she plopped a gigantic artichoke on my head, which I refused to wear: it made me easily 1.90 meters tall. She replaced it with a pair of braids that made me look like a little girl; the children squealed with joy. Then, in response to my hesitation, she arranged a single braid and added a kind of fringe across my forehead. The children lost it and I kept this hairdo, since they liked it so much. I fastened the stiletto heels Solange had her heart set on, while making sure to hide a good forgiving pair of short-heeled sandals, much more pleasant to wear, in my bag. Before leaving, I hid my fish eyes under sunglasses, but the rest I had to tolerate. It started on the bus when the driver whistled as I climbed into his vehicle. The woman who had given me an appointment told me plainly that she hadn't pictured me this way, she had imagined me more conservative and sensibly dressed. But Solange was to blame, I couldn't explain it, and I took the compliments in stride. Every store window shouted *quo vadis* at me. I took off those damn shoes to be more comfortable, and I hurried into the metro so there would be fewer eyes on me. I was already savoring the emotion that I felt each time I stood opposite the Montmartre basilica when a small man sitting next to me started to press his leg against mine while attentively reading a newspaper. I moved away as much as I could, the little man's callously indiscreet leg immediately inched toward the edge of my knee peeking out from my dress. I grabbed one of my kids and sat him across my lap, so the small man had a small pair of feet to entertain him throughout the trip, which he tried in vain to avoid. I saw that he was furious, but it amused me to no end.

I got off at Blanche, my kids were too hot, carrying their jackets in their arms. I had told them all about the funicular that goes up to the basilica and I pointed it out to them; they all had their noses in the air. They were looking for where the lift stops and, victoriously, one of them announced: "Look! It's not even as high as the one at la Bonne Mère!" He voiced his opinion clearly and audibly. While the others agreed, their sister was being photographed by a group of tourists. I snatched them away from the funicular entrance to plant them opposite the harmonious assemblage of stairs that lead to the basilica. They stopped for a minute to look;

how I'd love for them to see all that is beautiful in Paris! The youngest said: "We could sit over there! There are so many birds!" He hurried toward a very green lawn where brown birds were pecking. My happiness didn't last long, because the devil of the group broke the spell. Pointing at the majestic surroundings, he said, "This would be a great place to play tag, wouldn't it?"

And their sister added: "Hey, maman! Why aren't there umbrella pines like on the hill of Notre-Dame de la Garde? Where will we sit to eat?"

The one who wanted to play tag took charge of the operation and in a few leaps had climbed half the stairs, immediately followed by his three brothers. There were too many visitors, I knew it was pointless to call them, I didn't dare chase after them either; my skirt was too tight and too short. Above, dressed in matching red shirts like poppies in summer, my children watched me make the painful climb. Waving wildly at me, they seemed as overjoyed as if they had just conquered Mount Everest. They had also conquered a man who sold photos of the basilica at a prohibitive price. Of course, the kids already wanted to buy souvenirs. I distracted them from the man by pointing out a beige double-decker bus crammed with tourists.

They were too restless. Before we entered the basilica, I had to give them a short speech about piety. That's all it took, my dear Carolina, to get them to behave: a certain fear of God. I knew then that I could pray and bring them peacefully around that architectural marvel. And yet, my daughter whispered to me upon entering the church: "Why is it so dark?"

A woman with her camera hidden under a scarf was taking hasty photos. In the choir, people were on their knees praying. Everything was hushed and reverential. We decided to pray the rosary; I was on the twelfth bead when my kids finished theirs. They were intimidated and uncomfortable. The youngest discreetly tugged on the sleeves of my jacket. I kept going, concentrating as much as possible to ignore the heads spinning in every direction, the rosaries escaping under benches. I didn't cede to their desire to leave the church until one of the voices whispered: "Maman, we're hungry . . . " Near the doors to the basilica two nuns were collecting money, one of them old and wrinkled. The rebel of the gang who plays tag anywhere he can planted himself in front of the pitiful nun and said: "The poor thing! She must be terribly cold, what a shame! Why do they leave her here?"

When the why's and how's start to pour out, we have to find ingenious ways to extricate ourselves from the situation without seeming ignorant. I avoided it this time by replying: "It's almost noon, let's look for a shady corner to have our lunch."

We found a porch overlooking the small hill. We had climbed the steps leading there and were devouring our sandwiches when a group of thoroughly English-style boarders passed by. The young, respectably dressed girls, not meticulous but not disheveled, walked in an orderly fashion, flanked by two chaperones.

When they passed our group, they all cried out and came to a stop. A tribe of Black people eating on the basilica stairs was an unusual sight that certainly wasn't advertised in the leaflets on Montmartre. After negotiating with her students, a chaperone approached us and asked me in a typical accent if she could take a picture of us. The boys tried to act like movie stars, but the youngest flatly refused to be photographed, he hid his head between his folded arms. Then he grimaced so fiercely at the photographer that she left without further ado and rejoined her group amid their fits of laughter.

They had eaten and drunk their fill, and I delivered a short sermon to urge them to enter the basilica again: they would have as much time to sunbathe as they liked when they returned to Marseille. So we entered the church again; I wanted them to feast their eyes on those venerable stones, I wanted above all for them to remember at least one phrase from the numerous inscriptions indicating the origins of the grounds. They did a complete tour of the building, calmly and conscientiously reading everything I pointed out, and then promptly forgot it all as soon as we finally walked through the exit.

Chapter Fifteen

Postcards must be sent in the heat of the emotion caused by the beauty of things seen or heard, so I decided to write mine without delay. There was also a provocative motive to it. What's more amusing than writing these words to a woman who thinks you're rooted in a particular region: "From sunny Paris, sending my regards." I picture her throwing the little card into a wastepaper basket with contempt, or saying: "Now we've seen it all!" I picture my little old lady near Durance adjusting her glasses and calling her companions, her face beaming, her blue eyes misty with memories, waving my square card and crying: "My negress thinks of me! She will come visit me before winter." I picture Angèle throwing the elderly home into a tizzy, reading and rubbing her hands together from time to time: "The Martiniquan woman will bring me a medallion."

To write, I went back up the stairs to where we had eaten lunch; the kids who knew how to write were having a field day with their postcards as well. The two youngest had started a new game of tag, and so I had a moment of respite as they momentarily forgot to ask me questions beginning with "why."

It didn't last long; the baby wrested me from my tranquility with joyful cries: "Look! Maman! A Black priest! Black like us!"

Indeed, my eyes landed on a tall Black priest who was making his way up the hundred stairs not far from our group; he was reading a prayer book, what could be more natural? Jean-Pierre's words drew his attention. Visibly surprised, he walked toward us. The boys were already surrounding him: "Hello, father!"

His astonishment equaled mine. I put away my ballpoint pen and returned his greeting.

"Hello father! Have you come on a pilgrimage?"

"No," he answered, "I'm an apprentice here, I come from sub-Saharan Africa!"

"From Dakar, father? I know it! From Dahomey or Côte d'Ivoire? Those are marvelous countries!"

I listed the names of countries that had been French colonies, forgetting how immense the African continent is.

The priest answered: "No, I come from Belgian Congo!"

The children were overjoyed; for the first time in their lives, they were meeting a Black priest, they could speak to him, they could tell their Marseillais friends: "There's even a Black priest in Montmartre!"

It wouldn't be showing off, because it was true, it would be added to the list of things that they had seen, the Eiffel Tower, the big boulevards, the metro, and the "Parisian" breads. Furthermore, they were staring at the clergyman with much more interest than they had shown looking at the basilica itself, there was pride and curiosity in their eyes, they had stopped running around, they had stopped writing, they surrounded that man as if he were the most extraordinary being they had ever met. I was pleased; I asked the priest to tell me about the Congolese Church amid the revolution that was raging through the country. He was a witness of the end of an era, and what an era! He answered: "The Church has suffered from the events, but the population is profoundly religious, we yearn for peace . . . We wait . . . "

Then he inquired about me, my children. Did they all share the same father? They were so diversely colored! That question surprised me, but I answered: "Of course, father! They have the same dad! That's how it is in the West Indies! The children pick their color without consulting their parents, there's more race mixing than in Belgian Congo perhaps!"

The priest then asked me if I had already done a full tour of the basilica, I answered yes. Then the clergyman added: "Don't leave without showing your children the famous Place du Tertre. If you'd like, I can walk around with you. I'll go get ready, I'll be right back."

My dear Carolina, my pride knew no bounds, and this happens to me every time I meet a man of my race who has acceded to the priesthood. I was honored by his offer and did not refuse. I thought he was going to inform reception that he would be gone for a few minutes. I was wrong: getting ready meant putting his cassock away in a closet, because five minutes later, he came back in a well-tailored three-piece suit! He had the ease and stature of Sugar Ray.* I was slightly embarrassed. I didn't dare call this handsome man in his civilian clothes "Father" anymore. My enthusiasm fell flat. I said: "There you are, pastor!"

*Sugar Ray Robinson (1921–1989) was a Black American boxer whose career spanned from the 1940s to the 1960s.—Ed.

My children who always ask why said: “Maman, why is the priest wearing a disguise?”

I didn’t know why, but it didn’t please me one bit. We walked along a small street connecting the basilica to Place du Tertre. The painting sellers watched us pass nonchalantly. They didn’t bother to call out for customers; loud recordings came through cleverly hidden microphones and drew the attention of passersby. The priest rightfully pointed out to me that this avant-garde publicity contrasted with the antiquated square. The children, who had never seen so many paintings and painters in one place, dashed from one canvas to another, chattering. I was glad the priest had brought us there. Finally the little ones were faced with something completely new; they stopped talking about the Vieux Port. It also gave me something to talk about to dissolve the awkwardness that had taken hold once my priest had shown up “in civilian clothes.”

As we walked, an entire legion of people, of all races and languages, turned and stared.

A group of tourists stopped and I heard: “Look, a Black pastor, he has children!”

I noticed that the priest wore his collar like a Protestant and, lifting my head toward him, I also noticed he was staring with superhuman interest at the fish Solange had drawn on my face. My ears turned red and I searched in my weekend bag for the pair of black sunglasses buried in it. My eyes thus shielded, I mixed into the crowd strolling around the square. The priest had taken my youngest’s hand, he managed to ruin things by murmuring to me in a satisfied voice: “People think these are my children! Soon we’ll be able to get married!”

I pretended not to have heard, I found a way to get ahead of him by fixing the buckles of my daughter's sandals, even though they hadn't come undone. An icy shower cooled me down once and for all when one of the clergyman's well-groomed hands brushed against my bare arm. First my eyes, now I had to hide my arms in the nylon jacket I had taken off because it was so hot! I quickly buttoned myself up to the collar, with no remorse. The man who had turned back into an athlete had revealed his opinion on the matter of sexual tolerance among certain religious orders.

It really bothered me, it offended all the solid traditions that had been inculcated in me since childhood. I replied that the day when Catholics discovered in Bible study that this tolerance should be granted to priests, this would be the end of their faith, and I would be the first to be dismayed. For me, a priest is a living sacrifice; he mustn't cheat, especially not in thought. You're either a priest or you're not.

The clergyman told me to speak more quietly, that people might overhear what I was saying. I took refuge in a group admiring an artist who was cutting out silhouettes from black paper.

It irritated me, and I said that the men who serve my church shouldn't say anything that can't be shouted to the whole world.

My dear Carolina, what a hornet's nest! Imagine, that still wasn't enough to fluster my Sugar Ray, he offered candy to the children, spoke to me of the Moulin de la Galette and Montmartre by night.

I asked him the name of the Montmartre bells, and the church that was fifty steps from us. He didn't answer, but feasted his eyes on the Andalusian hairdo Solange had planted on my head. I put my braid up and hid it under the scarf that I pulled out of my bag. I was hot, too hot, covered up like this, but it didn't matter. I couldn't let anything in my appearance encourage the shocking attentions of this priest I had trusted.

My little girl was standing in front of the artist's easel. In a few seconds he had cut out a silhouette that looked rather like hers. The four boys jostled me: "Us too, maman, we want our heads!"

Good God, I thought, 50 francs apiece! That's reasonable. A moment later, the man who was dexterously cutting the paper turned to me and presented the silhouettes created by his agile hands: "Don't they look just like them? Only two thousand five hundred francs!" I was stunned, I didn't dare turn down this work I had asked for, but there's quite a difference between 250 and 2,500 francs! I rifled feverishly in my wallet and tried to gather enough money while the amused tourists watched the children jump for joy with their cutouts. How could I have been so mistaken? I looked more closely at the sign, where the price was listed as five francs. Not very helpful for those of us who can't ever manage to count properly in new francs, which must cause issues quite often.

I had 1,500 francs left for the day. I had bought altar candles, postcards, put money in all the basilica's collection boxes; I thought that for the first time I had been able to save a bit of the funds allocated for my day as an amateur tourist and I was now faced with a cruel reality. I had to ask the kids to empty their wallets to collect enough for these pieces of black paper. The clergyman understood my predicament, he quickly offered to pay. I was wary and refused without regret. I told the artist that I had gotten the price wrong, that he could keep two of the paper cut-outs. I gave him all my pocket money and returned the designs I couldn't pay for. The priest took them back from him and paid, then handed them to the children, who were delighted that they wouldn't be deprived of their costly souvenirs.

The priest appeared to have returned to reason, he chatted with the children, he seemed to forget my presence; I was relieved but I thought it was time to be off, because my daughter was once again posing in front of an artist who painted colorful portraits. I promised a pair of slaps to the docile model if she didn't scram right away. The clergyman showed me the ancient post office at the top of the hill and started to speak of everything but religion. He became too relaxed again, I had to do something, for the sake of my faith that he was rattling with his ordinary-man talk. My kid who was still playing tag was clinging to the man; he extended his hand as if to a friend and started eyeing me fiercely again. Enough was enough. I pulled a few postcards from my bag and told the children I was going to mail them. The clergyman realized that I was trying to get rid of him. He didn't accept defeat; he answered that he needed to buy some stamps. He didn't let go of Jean-Pierre. When the clergyman had entered the post office, I said to my kid in patois: "Let go of the priest! Come see this artist!" The priest got in line to buy some stamps. Jean-Pierre let go of him and came back to me. I said to the kids: "We're leaving, quickly, it's late, already four o'clock! The priest needs to say Vespers, he'll have to get dressed properly now, we don't have time to attend the service, you're exhausted!"

I hurried down the road. Bypassing Place du Tertre, I brought my kids to the Moulin de la Galette. I stopped for a minute to uncover my arms, which were burning up under my synthetic-fiber jacket. I removed the silk scarf and sunglasses, I wiped my brow, which had transformed into a river: Solange's little fish, all damp, were not pleased. I was tense. He had made a mockery of what was most dear to me: my faith and my race. Why had Solange styled me in such a misleading way that a priest had let himself be ensnared? I blamed Solange, which calmed me down. The kids looked back, one of them shouted: "Maman, there's the priest, he's looking for us, look maman! Why can't we say goodbye to him?"

Indeed, from the top of rue Lepic, I saw the lofty stature of the elegant Black man. He was moving through the crowd, suddenly he looked toward the windmill and spotted our group. The children raised their arms, I started to retreat; it saved me, and the self-respect that should never have left him won out perhaps, he raised his large arms and waved goodbye, he didn't follow us. I was satisfied, I was delivered. Perhaps, I thought, he was going to fetch his prayer book. Picturing the priest reading the words of wisdom of the One he is supposed to serve comforted me; by fleeing, by speaking to him harshly, I felt as if I had saved him from himself. Saving ourselves from ourselves is a terrible battle, one we can only wage on our own.

I couldn't explain that to my kid who was walking back. I answered: "We can't say goodbye! We have to leave him alone, he told me the sun was giving him a migraine!"

The greengrocers had cleared off of rue Lepic. Here and there, pigeons abandoned the gray roofs for the sidewalk to find their pittance. A plum seller stood in front of a handcart. The children hurtled down the road and camped in front of the meager display of wine-colored fruit, which had become sticky from the heat. They reached into their wallets and procured an ample provision of plums: "Finally," they declared, "something that isn't more expensive than in Marseille!"

The one always playing tag, the romantic of the group, spun his paper silhouette around and around in its plastic bag: "He was kind, the Black priest! Too bad he's not coming with us!"

We'll never see him again, he won't ever come. As I spoke those words, the metro was waiting for us at Blanche. I rushed through the doors. Now, we had left Montmartre behind for good.

In the car where we had taken our place, a terribly sad Black girl watched my kids. I was struck by the expression of lassitude the Blacks in Paris have, even in summer when there is the sun that they should never be without.

I made a detour at Quai de la Rapée, where Yolande lives, opposite the Seine. It's been a year since she became a Parisian and started bragging to me about her new life. She dared to take the bus and visit the Palace of Versailles. I looked for the entrance to her place, but I saw only a small bistro where a customer in a baseball cap was leaning against the counter.

"Mademoiselle Yolande?" I asked the woman working there. My children, intrigued, waited.

"Mademoiselle Yolande? Third floor on the left. You enter through here."

I realized that to enter the building you had to go through the bistro. I pressed a timer light switch in vain. I felt for the stairs; in the tortuous stairwell we stubbed our toes against the loose tiles. Finally we were on the third floor, but I couldn't distinguish left from right. I knocked on every door. An old woman helped me: "The West Indians?

Two doors down." She immediately slammed the door in my face, and I was in darkness once more. I called: "Mademoiselle Yolande! Mademoiselle Yolande!"

A door opened a crack. A girl I didn't recognize told me to enter. Once I was inside with my five children, the room was more packed than Place de l'Étoile on the fourteenth of July. The girl stared at us, bewildered: "I'm looking for Yolande, I'm from Marseille, I'd like to see her before I go back." The girl wanted to tell us to sit down, but she only had two chairs, I could see she was embarrassed. I learned that Yolande had two days off, that she had gone to Le Havre for Assumption Day weekend. I also learned that three girls shared this glorified closet, so whenever they had the chance, one of them would leave. I was shocked that guests had to pass through the bistro. The girl told me that that's how it was and that many times the owner, depending on her mood, announced that such and such of her tenants was absent even when it wasn't the case. She concluded by saying: "We can't have it all, work and housing. I'm leaving soon, I have enough saved for key money, I was promised a room in Faubourg Saint-Antoine, only 150,000 francs, and then I'll only have to pay 9,000 francs a month in rent." For her, this was El Dorado. I told her that was great, and walked back to the stairs with my children. This time, the girl illuminated our steps with a battery-operated lamp. It was five o'clock and Quai de la Rapée was deserted in this area. We walked from there to Gare de Lyon so I could buy our return tickets.

Oh yes, Carolina, it's time for us to return, there's nothing left for me to do but pack up my manuscript and my illusions in my suitcase and return to my fair city of Marseille to finish my vacation or begin my rentrée. I already have to start planning for the return to school.

Tonight as I write to you, the children sleep, wrecked with fatigue but happy. Solange came home at one in the morning. She kicked off her high heels and said:

"So, your makeup, my dear? Was it a success?"

"Yes," I answered, "with a Congolese priest."

Solange forgot her fatigue, she let out an immense and irrepressible laugh that woke up the kids. Her joy won me over and, as she helped me pack the suitcases, I forgot the sadness that had taken hold at the end of that memorable day.

This trip that I had anticipated for so long was now complete, my vacation was over, all that was left was my children's joy and, at the bottom of my shopping bag, my intact manuscript that will return to its origins.

The return trip is set for tomorrow afternoon, I'll get some rest and forget how twisted the world is. From her bedroom, half asleep, Solange said to me: "You know, not to discourage you, but you shouldn't get your hopes up for your book, or any future books! Better to have a good job that brings in money! That way, no one knows you, you just have loads of cash to spend! What do you think about us buying a little restaurant together? I'll put down the money and you'll help me! People eat every day: we'll make merguez for the North Africans, spring rolls for the Vietnamese, and fish soup for the West Indians! It would be terrific! But books, you know, people don't read every day, we don't buy books all the time! And you have to pull all-nighters to write them! Whereas grub! Everyone has to eat! Don't get too hung up on it." She yawned, the rest of her babbling got lost in the shadows.

This harsh common sense did me a world of good and tonight, Carolina, I am fully convinced that Solange is right.

Chapter Sixteen

August 16, 1963

My husband was waiting for me at the train station the day before yesterday, the children thronged him to tell him about everything pell-mell: the big boulevards, the Black priest, and the mistral that had overtaken us on the way. All day yesterday I avoided speaking about my tour of the publishing houses. But he asked me this afternoon:

"So, my writer, how's it going? I went to Cannes with some friends, I saw all the book and film people bronzing themselves on the beaches! You would have been better off going to the coast to find an editor!"

"Oh yes, you know, of course, everything is closed up there!"

I was almost happy that all the houses had been closed; that way, I didn't have to tell him that they had rejected my manuscript, because he would have immediately retorted: "You see, I was right!"

And yes! He is right, Carolina! And Solange is right! But now that I've got a bee in my bonnet, just try and get it out! I manage to forget while I shake out the ladies' rugs, and then, despite myself, I unearth an old notebook and scribble some words. For now, it's out of the question: the washing machine is full to bursting, my husband confessed that he doesn't know how to use it! I have an incredible amount of tidying to do in the closets and there's dust heaped in every corner. The potatoes that I left in a crate have sprouted and the fridge is frosted over. We exhaust ourselves to leave and then exhaust ourselves to resume the normal course of life. The sun is still just as hot and the cicadas chant like mad!

All the same, I'd really like to know why he went to Cannes, when I thought he was quite sick of his tribe. It'll be like pulling teeth to get it out of him, but in the meantime, so many things to do in the house! And the restless children are already hatching a plan to go to the beach. Given how limp our purse is after our trip, they'll have to wait till the end of the month to visit the Calanques.

August 18, 1963

An odd guy showed up and asked for my husband, he was wearing white linen pants and a pink shirt! I learned that he was from Guadeloupe and had just arrived in Marseille, he didn't want to say any more to me, he waited two hours in front of the door because I couldn't convince him to come in and sit down. The children, just as intrigued as me, circled around him and embarrassed him tremendously.

Finally I watched him take off in long strides; he had caught sight of my husband in the distance, he didn't have the patience to wait for him any longer. My husband literally pushed him inside the apartment. The young man obstinately stared at his leather sandals. I said: "What is this man's problem?"

My husband replied, deadpan:

"He's a stowaway we found in Cannes."

"Who is 'we'?"

Suddenly, I understood why my husband had been acting strange since my return, because then he added:

"Well, yes! You remember, I told you I was in Cannes. It was to disembark a family of Martiniquans: a postwoman and four children, the wife of a colleague who brought me along . . ."

"And?"

"And this boy arrived clandestinely on the *Irpina*! I was at the quay when I spotted him with a group of soldiers who had also jumped off the speedboat, one of them told us about this boy's counterfeit situation. It was serious, the customs officers were there, and the French National Police were inspecting passports a hundred meters away. The soldiers told me and my colleague that they had fed him and dressed him on the boat, for a bit of fun. They had even gotten him onto the speedboat. But now that they were in France, they thought that the game had gone on long enough. The stowaway approached us and asked if he could cross the quay in our company. He took one of my coworker's children by the hand and headed calmly for the jetty. I told him that if he managed to get out of it, so much the better, but not to involve us in his mess. I chewed him out rather loudly, people were staring. Thankfully I was speaking in patois. We had been there since eight in the morning and the customs officers had already seen us, the French National Police had probably taken note of the people there waiting for the passengers. With his pink shirt I imagined he wouldn't get very far. My friend had taken off his gray jacket, it was too hot, it was already eleven o'clock when the *Irpina* arrived . . ."

"And! What happened next, papa!"

The children had approached, they were eyeballing the boy who was still stubbornly staring at his sandals. I had brought him a cup of coffee and a tartine, he was eating and seemed to be in his own world. He was probably reliving the scene; beads of sweat decorated his forehead. A stowaway passenger! The boys couldn't believe their ears! A hero from an adventure tale in the flesh, and under their roof. I sensed that they wanted to interrogate him, it would be intrusive and perhaps even burdensome for this man. I shooed the kids away and my husband continued: "A soldier who had already passed through customs yelled: 'Monsieur! Monsieur! Lend this little namby-pamby your jacket or he'll be sent straight to the police station.' My colleague handed over his jacket, he didn't need to be told twice. The boy put it on and made the sign of the cross!"

Now I understood the embarrassment of this tall fellow in his pink shirt. He was emotional, he set down the cup and his tongue came untied, he lifted his forehead and said: "I was resigned, the hardest part was getting through the boat landing. The lady's children were near me, I took one in my arms and spoke to him; as we passed by the gendarmes, I said: 'So, you didn't get seasick?' The soldiers in the distance watched me cross the barrier, the child's parents were with the customs officers who were marking the luggage that had already been inspected, I put the kid down and stepped onto the sidewalk, I didn't know where to go. I asked your husband how to get to Fréjus. I have a brother who is, or rather who was, in Camp Robert, the soldiers took me for a bite near the Cannes train station and your husband bought me a train ticket to Fréjus, he was kind enough to give me your address and told me to come see him one day."

That day seemed to have arrived pretty quickly. I asked: "And your brother?"

The boy took a piece of paper from his pocket and resumed his story: "He's in Bourges; I found that out once I arrived at Camp Robert. Is Bourges far from here?"

I was puzzled; I asked why he had dared to leave illegally with no passenger ticket, no luggage, seemingly no plan . . .

He answered:

"I wanted to be in the army, but they put me on *congé budgétaire,* so I couldn't go.* The factory where I was working laid off its employees. I applied to an accelerated vocational school, but I failed the exam. I was told that in France, the exams aren't as difficult. So I tried my luck!"

"Your luck! But don't you realize how difficult it will be for you to find your bearings? You don't have money, and Bourges isn't close by! Even if it were, do you think that your brother, with no warning of your arrival, would be able to help you right away?"

My dear Carolina, when we have nothing, it's right now that counts: rose-colored glasses won't help us when we're in dire straits.

My husband had joined me in the kitchen, he didn't know what to tell me; I was more troubled than angry. He scratched his head and said:

*Citizens of France's overseas territories, including the West Indies, were typically unable to serve or were excused from service in the French army or navy due to lack of need or due to their distance from mainland France.—Tr.

"I can't believe it! I never thought I would see him again and here he is: what should we do with him?"

"We'll give him a clean shirt and pants, I'm sure his used to be white. We'll give him some food, and in the meantime you figure something out!"

My husband seemed delighted; he knew he could count on me.

In Fréjus, the soldiers had given the boy an address in Harlem; when he was done eating, that's where he wanted to go. He was almost guaranteed to run into a police checkpoint; all of Marseille's unsavory characters hang out there. The stowaway seemed unaware of this, he had an identity card but no certificate of residence, and he was supposed to be living on rue Frébault in Pointe-à-Pitre; even so, I couldn't just adopt him, I already had enough on my plate with my family and the money for the rest of the month gobbled up! I also couldn't, in good conscience, let him go to Harlem: he didn't seem like a thug.

While I was thinking about what to do, he emerged from the bathroom where my husband had brought him. Nicely shaven and coiffed, he seemed even more confident than before he'd gone in. He said: "You are like a mother to me, God bless you!" His mother! Well then! God had inspired my husband, but I was still aggravated! My husband knew it, he said to me in front of the boy: "I'll go find the address of a night shelter, I'll bring him to town, and we'll see . . ."

The boy thanked me again and jumped on the back of my husband's moped. One of the kids who was watching through the window cried: "That's it, papa's stowaway is gone!"

I awaited my husband's return late into the night; he was able to find a place in a shelter for the boy in the pink shirt: he could only stay there for the night and had to skedaddle at dawn to find work. I let out a sigh of relief knowing that the boy had shelter for the night. As each day brings its seed to the birds, I sincerely hope that Providence will not forget him.

August 18, 1963

Cécile is full of hope, she writes and tells me how happy she is to be expecting a boy, because it will be a boy, she claims. She also wants to know if I've managed to find an editor. This whole thing is rather embarrassing. I wish I could forget it once and for all. But what I can't forget is back-to-school season and the costs that go along with it. I'm already thinking about finding a job, because I want all the kids to have the famous nylon smocks they so covet.

August 20, 1963

The stowaway returned this afternoon to ask us for a residence certificate in order to register with the labor force. He also asked us to make a request on his behalf to enroll in an accelerated vocational school; he didn't have to beg, we were all too happy to see him on the right path. The boy also wrote to his brother. He finds it difficult to sleep at the night shelter, worse than on the boat. Apparently two other guests fought right next to his bed, the police had to come quiet things down. He's having such a rude awakening that he already misses his home country. He walked the ten kilometers from town to our house, he has no more money. And even if he did, he confessed that he doesn't know how to use the bus tickets. He didn't take shortcuts; all along the road, he asked people: "Does the nine pass through here?" and he followed all the meanderings of the nine bus. He says that he's starting to get the hang of it: he had come on foot the first time, too. I hadn't realized this, and the boy became even more interesting to me; when he arrived in Marseille, he could have mixed in with the riffraff, but he chose to follow the bus line leading to a family that resembled his own and might be able to give him some advice. When he told us this, he could see from our smiles that he had become one of us. So, my dear Carolina, I did what I hope someone might do one day for one of my kids. I offered to accompany him to the employment office tomorrow. My husband wouldn't have been able to bring him for another week, he needs to earn our bread. I don't know whether the boy would be brave enough to navigate the process on his own; I can picture him visiting the offices without ever daring to enter, out of timidity, out of fear: it's his first direct contact with Europeans. There were, of course, many gendarmes in Guadeloupe, but you don't have friendly relations with them there, even if they're your next-door neighbor. There were also two white priests in his neighborhood, but he thinks they're Canadian. He also tells us that over there, the postwar Europeans have become a real pain, somewhat racist and arrogant. Those before the maelstrom of 1939 who came to the colony were more accepting and even protective. When the boy doesn't feel observed, he speaks freely; I stop myself from asking questions because if I do, he looks at his feet and clams up; I move from one room to another while he speaks, it puts him more at ease. I brought him up to speed by explaining to him that fortunately in France, an office worker is an office worker, a bit melancholy in Marseille, it's true, but not "the European at the counter" from back home who thinks he's descended from Mount Olympus. He doesn't dare believe it yet. So I decided to bring him tomorrow.

August 22, 1965

When I returned at noon, my youngest told me triumphantly that the collector from the electric company had come by, he had explained to the man that maman had left to meet papa's stowaway. I had to put a stop to this term, because the boy is no longer a stowaway, except in his conscience. I got him a job as a handler at a sparkling water factory. Everyone is thirsty this time of year and they need a lot of personnel in places that bottle refreshing beverages.

I entered the employment office very early in the morning, the boy had followed my instructions and was waiting for me at my bus stop. I immediately spotted him because he was wearing his pink shirt. In vain, I tried to boost his confidence as we made our way to the house of hope. He kept staring at his feet. I told him that he had to relax because, despite his stature, with his gloomy expression people would be hesitant to hire him.

My efforts were futile; after we had stood in line and our turn had finally come to enter the office reserved for handling jobs, despite the employee's affability, the boy in pink couldn't utter a single syllable. I quickly remedied the situation by explaining that he had just arrived, that he wasn't familiar with the formalities of registering with the offices. After all, I couldn't say that he was afraid of Europeans and was waiting to be treated with disdain like in the West Indies.

I asked the employee to find him something as soon as possible.

He was wonderful, the man at the counter! He scratched his ear, searched in the registers for quite a long time, and finally said: "Okay, here's what you'll do: bring this form to this factory, they're hiring! With the nice weather, you'll be able to work up to twelve hours per day."

The hands of the boy in pink trembled, he read and reread the rectangular paper the employee had given him. Without a word, he extended his large hand. The employee, who had seen others like him, simply said: "Good luck. If it doesn't work out, come back and see me!"

My mission wasn't complete, I climbed the stairs that led me to the career guidance office. Strangely, and fortunately for my protégé, all the people I encountered this morning were totally charming.

A Black man had preceded us, which allowed me to say to the boy: "You see, we're not the only ones!"

The smiling woman who greeted us had a kind face, but it didn't stop my boy from staring at his feet. I was starting to get used to it; I explained that the boy wanted to enroll in a vocational school that would also give him housing. Without missing a beat, the employee said: "The exam will take place in September, you've come at the right time, you won't have to wait long. The apprenticeship will begin immediately after. I don't know where you'll be placed, fill out this form." To my great surprise, I noticed that he had neat handwriting and I learned that he had his driver's license.

His face lit up with a happy smile when I told him that we were going to the factory right away. We changed buses and neighborhoods again.

After arriving, I presented the voucher that my protégé had handed to me. He was fretful and anxious. Hiring season had ended a long time ago, but this morning was his lucky day, because the head supervisor was registering the new arrivals. I told him that we lived quite far from town, that "my younger brother" had just arrived and it was his first job in France. The supervisor removed his glasses and seemed intrigued. He gave orders to a secretary: "Give him a sheet, he's starting now! He'll clock in this afternoon, you'll only do two hours this morning. Does that work for you?"

The boy stammered a few words, he followed the supervisor and the automatic doors of an immense, noisy hall closed behind him.

Of course, today my family did not have any stew for lunch. I made pasta to save time and the tournedos were only half-cooked. No one at the table grimaced, we were too busy talking about the boy in pink and, at the end of our improvised meal, we were as delighted as if we had just won the lottery. It's our conscience, Carolina! Today, mine testifies to me and I'm almost ashamed at feeling so light despite my empty purse. I say: "My God, let it be joy, but not pride, otherwise my actions will have no meaning." As for my husband, I know that he shares my sentiment because he didn't even say to me: "Pasta, in this heat!"

August 30, 1963

The boy's brother came from Bourges; he was able to take leave and came straight to my house. They look shockingly alike. He didn't seem to be proud of his younger brother. I reassured him of his brother's conduct and told him how "our stowaway" had gotten to work diligently. Apparently he works fourteen-hour days, he sent us a note that I showed to the officer. He was relieved, but even so he murmured: "If he'd been taken on arrival, and if he'd been thrown in prison, my mother would have died; she's been sick since he left, she realized what he had done because he brought nothing with him. She's sending his suitcase to our address."

The boy, who will no longer be in pink now, asked us in his letter to find him a small room. He gets back to the shelter too late at night to be let in, so he has an arrangement with a night guard and shares his room, but it's only temporary, because such things are forbidden by management. He added: "I was wrong, not all Europeans are unapproachable, I don't know why they're like that back home!"

So much the better! May his euphoria last!

September 4, 1963

I've been taking it easy for a few days now, unburdened by thoughts, the worries will have plenty of time to arrive with winter and the start of school. Yesterday I even took a bath . . . in oil! There were so many people roasting in the sun that I had to wait until sunset to don my bathing suit. When I entered the grayish substance bringing joy to all those vacationers, it was already cold, despite the relentless sun that was still scorching the tanning fanatics. In a few moments, I managed to snag a corner of rock that a couple had just left. I realized that I was all slimy, and I understood immediately why there were no swimmers in this area. Some kind of accident had caused a wave to bring a slick of gasoline to that very spot. I returned to the beach and heard a large woman tell her family: "It's true what they say, all the oil tankers of Mourepiane piss in the current near the rocks! Hey, sweetie! You won't smell like roses after swimming over there!"

There was nothing to do but rush home and thoroughly scrub myself. Two bus rides with the crazed, tired, but satisfied children, and then I wouldn't smell like an oil depot anymore. Carolina, we have to be careful when we go in the water around Marseille! People dive at Pointe-Rouge and bring back to the surface all sorts of debris, empty cans, dead cats, enough to drive away even the most sea-obsessed!

You have to be in the know about which places are not yet infested with oil or trash, or else settle for tanning! Tanning! That awful word that throws whites into a frenzy! Naturally tan, I carefully avoid exposing myself to the sun out of fear of "sunstroke," and I am always flabbergasted by the sight of those people roasting in the heat. There's such a thing as too much sun!

This is what I call taking it easy, and it could have lasted, but this morning an impeccably dressed man in a splendid summer suit came to visit me. I was surprised when he announced that he was the literary agent from rue Saint-Sulpice. He was passing through Marseille and had come to see me out of curiosity. I was peeling potatoes; the children wanted fries, and plenty of them, they said. I opened the door with one hand, firmly holding a potato in the other. He seemed astonished when I told him that I was in fact the woman of letters who had written to him, but it didn't last long. I told him that I didn't have a penny to invest in a literary project that might amount to nothing.

So he asked me what I was working on now. I said:

"Uh . . . well . . . I'm writing to Carolina!"

"Who is Carolina?" he asked.

My dear, in the time since I started writing to you, I've managed to forget the name of your village, but I answered: "A South American woman! You know! Do you want to see a few pages?"

He delved into my scribbling while I prepared a punch, he was fully absorbed. When I saw that he was smiling, I got embarrassed. He finally cried: "How unusual! I haven't read anything like it! You must turn it into a manuscript!"

He wasn't kidding, he even told me to hurry up and do it quickly. But I'm not in a rush, because it will be the same story, no cash for such a thing, whether it be now or in ten years . . .

September 8, 1963

It hasn't even been two weeks since he arrived in Europe and our protégé already seems to be gaining confidence. He came to see us and brought me a bunch of flowers. He is happy because he found a small room in the suburbs near the factory where he works. He no longer looks stubbornly at his feet, he forms plans, he tells us what happens in the hangar where he handles bottles. He showed us a small photo of a Mediterranean-looking girl and said with a smile: "We're going to the ball together, she works near me, her family is Armenian!"

When he left, my husband said: "We don't have to worry about him anymore, there is nothing better to help a boy like him find his way than a native girl who lends a hand . . . " Of course, I wasn't entirely in agreement with him, but better that for the boy than the gang in Harlem.

September 10, 1963

I went around to the shops and I'm full of dread because I have so much to buy. Sooner or later I'll have to find a job, despite my husband's shouts.

September 12, 1963

The International Fair will be open for twelve days. A good tenth of the women will flock there, a good handful of students too, in search of relatively easy temporary work. My Guadeloupean compatriot, who has quite a few tricks up her sleeve, told me that she was a dishwasher in a restaurant at the fair, a terrific job, no ladies, no men of the house who sniff the plates to check whether or not they smell like fish. You plunge the dish in soapy water, you rinse it, often it dries on its own. "The best part," she told me, "is that it's the same men who flock here to eat off of this dubious dishware." She added, "And when the time comes, I can get hired anywhere; as a demonstrator, as a saleswoman or a handler." I'll go tomorrow; I'm not leaving the house on a whim, but out of necessity. I don't think there are many mothers who leave their brood on a whim when they're in my situation. In any event, there are no two ways about it, I have two hands and I have to make use of them. I only type with six fingers, maybe that's why my pages don't sustain me, so I will use all ten fingers, my dear Carolina, and diligently, if I don't want to be caught unprepared, because here comes autumn. Between two hot days, a cool gust announces that summer is slipping away. The shrubs have lost their flowers and the cherries can only be found crystallized in tins. There are grapes everywhere, the harvest is close at hand; once more that damn winter will send shivers down my carcass that can't acclimate to the cold. Already, already . . . if I could stay home when the mistral makes the people of Provence walk at a slant, I would call myself privileged. This is why, while there's still time, I have to anticipate the purchase of extra shoes and comfortable anoraks. I'll go earn my bread, as they say to men, with the sweat on my brow. It's a necessity, and feeling useless when I can bring home three francs per hour torments me. I will go to the fair. Besides, I'm not the only one: the Blacks who come en masse shouldn't delude themselves, there's only a Salvador or a Baker once every twenty years,* and they need to be resilient enough not to get swept up in the whirlwind. Since autumn has arrived, all the Black moms will leave their furnished apartments, their hotel rooms, they'll put their children in the school canteen, in the nursery, they'll go to the factory, to ladies' homes, at least that's

*Henri Salvador (1917–2008) was born in Cayenne, French Guiana, and arrived in France in 1929. He was an author, composer, performer, comedian, and musician.—Ed.

how it is in Marseille. The date factories will snatch up a fair amount of them, the cookie factories will also take a few, and when all those women have amassed enough money to send a package to those who stayed back home, they will have the pride, courage, or nerve, depending on your perspective, to write to their family: "I'm doing well, I hit the jackpot." Then others will come by the boatload and from every port, and then they too will get caught up in the cycle, and they will begin to think of winter after winter, always the same. It changes nothing to write to you, but it helps to be able to understand why my sisters seem sadder in winter.

There is something else I noticed that never ceases to amaze me: when a mainlander, no matter her social rank, arrives in the West Indies or in a Third World country, she is bound for a better life. The farm girls become executive secretaries, the cleaning women are immediately transformed into important ladies. Those who had only ever seen a bank in pictures work in them; if they don't know how to write, they sort banknotes. So when we know how to speak French, we tell ourselves that when we arrive in Europe, we'll be saleswomen in department stores, or secretaries if we know how to write a letter properly. But I will never cease to be astounded by the chasm between dream and reality.

There you have it, all this on top of the cold wind depresses me, and to chase that feeling away, there is nothing better than the Foire de Marseille.

September 14, 1963

I went to the employment office in Parc Chanot: I was told to come back on the seventeenth. I won't miss it.

September 16, 1963

Our protégé is ecstatic, he has been summoned for a physical aptitude test on rue Sylvabelle. His happiness is infectious.

September 17, 1963

I walked all over the little town that is Parc Chanot. A caretaker let me into the park because he remembered my face, he wished me luck finding a job. Meanwhile, a gigantic queue of women of all ages waited patiently for the employment office to call upon their services. When the boy signaled to me, it caused a commotion in the crowd:

"I was here first!"

"I've come here three days in a row!"

"Unbelievable!"

I restrained myself from responding; the boy would be embarrassed if his act provoked a small war. He yelled: "She's not waiting in line, she has a stall! Hurry up, your family is waiting for you at the West Indies stall!"

I had no fairground family that I knew of, but I looked for the West Indies stall from one end of the fair to the other. Fortunately I had made sure to pack a spare pair of sandals, the large handbag trend is useful for something at least; I can stash my high heels at any moment. I stopped to check out the food mill demonstrators, the yogurt sellers, the farm equipment handlers, the booksellers and the coffee sellers—in vain! I roamed the stalls of fledgling states, I chatted up a Black diplomat who explained that most countries delegated knowledgeable representatives to speak about the things on display. I also visited the beekeepers and the horticulturalists, but I didn't have the right accent to speak of honey and lavender in Provence, so I ordered a Coca-Cola on the terrace of a large ale house and took the opportunity to ask the server whether his establishment was hiring dishwashers or saleswomen. "The full-time positions are filled," he answered, "but go over to the outdoor market, where the sandwich sellers are." I introduced myself to a person selling ham from Auvergne, someone selling charcuterie from Bretagne, and the man displaying salami from Lyon. I spoke to the people making crêpes Normandy style, and those selling merry-making wines: they didn't even look at me before saying: "No, not hiring." Sometimes other women also looking for a job crossed my path and asked me: "So, have you found anything?"

I answered no and we tried to encourage each other, maybe later . . . Maybe over there by the souks! . . . It's possible that they'll need people tomorrow morning in the beer halls . . . We knew they were just empty words, but we said them anyway to forget the kilometers we'd walked through the dusty alleyways. Then I rested in the shade of a large plane tree. And there, behind that large tree, I heard men speaking Creole. One of them said: "Heavens! I would love a West Indian woman in the stall this year."

I held my breath, because the other added: "They're not hard to find, in the eight days I've been here I've seen a good dozen looking for work."

I let them leave and followed them at a distance to find this providential stand that was at last looking to hire a Black woman. The two men entered the wooden shack that hadn't yet been assembled, a heap of ladders, crates and boxes of all kinds encumbering the place.

I presented myself confidently and declared: "You're looking for a saleswoman, I believe? Have you already found one?"

My compatriot broke into a big smile and cried out: "No! Do you have someone for me?"

I was surprised, but I managed to inform him that I was the one looking for work.

The man eyeballed my gloves and my elegant outfit!

I had donned my prettiest summer dress. He said: "I figured you had your own stall, I saw you pass by earlier, not for a minute did I imagine that you were looking for a job. What is your name? Maybe I know your family?"

How nice; finally, an employer who asks my identity! Then he announced that I would start at that very moment. And so begins one more parenthetical in this year that had been coming to a close.

September 18, 1963

I spoke nonstop for twelve hours, and I'm supposed to do this for twelve days? I don't know how many times I repeated: "Have a look, messieurs-dames! A little look at the spices. Come and grab some spices!"

I repeated these words in front of a mountain of tubes filled with evocatively named ingredients: Guadeloupe vanilla, Jamaican chili, Indian curry, Madagascar saffron, Algerian harissa, Martinique cinnamon. You can find these things all over Marseille, but there is so much excitement at the fairs that you can push anything on anyone as long as you know how to sell it. A hundred times I explained how to make curried rice to the "customers" who, after listening, left the merchandise with me, citing indigestion! When the boss isn't there, it's a piece of cake, I just have to make my pitch to other customers, and provide recipes for Ceylon tea or fish soup with saffron; but when the boss is there, I have to squeeze a few purchases out of the customers. Otherwise, he furrows his brow and taps on the counter nervously: "In Marseille, it's always like this! People come to walk around and not to buy anything! Figure out how to discern the serious customers!"

My dear Carolina, that's all I did all day, and the boss thanked me before I took my leave tonight.

September 19, 1963

Renée, walking just behind her employers, passed by my stall. She came to say hello to me, slightly embarrassed, while they were staring at the heap of Turkish delight that I had just displayed near a pile of other Oriental products. When they heard Renée speak, they looked in my direction, and the woman cried as if I weren't there: "That's the one who replaced Renée, she's a saleswoman now!!!"

I spoke to Renée without looking at the lady. "So, you're still working for those pigs?"

Renée hunched her back and followed them without reacting; furiously, I gave my spiel: "Over here, messieurs-dames, a whole assortment of spices, all the products of the colonies!" I watched Renée's resigned silhouette blend into the crowd. Then an amused voice made me turn my head: "Don't say all the products from the colonies! Say: all the products from the overseas territories." It was a nuance, and we were only talking about cinnamon; meanwhile, opposite me, a living colonial product was glumly trailing behind her intransigent employers. I went silent, so my employer asked me: "I don't mean to vex you, but now we only say 'overseas territories,' the rest doesn't exist."

The rest doesn't exist! He doesn't know about the rest that remains for my sisters! And for how much longer?

The mistral started to blow and it whipped whirlwinds of dust onto the display. I used coconuts to keep down the newspaper that sheltered from the sun a few tubes of vanilla that had crystallized from the heat.

And Renée, this time, rushed over to me to say: "I finished paying for my trip this month! I'll be able to give my notice!"

I didn't even look at her, for fear she might recant her words. The stall owner was there, it was a good excuse not to respond, because I am forbidden from wasting time with people who have no intention of buying anything.

The rain followed the mistral and, early this evening, the alleyways of the park were deserted, the harried crowd mobbed the buses and taxis parked nearby. Water seeped through my blouse and I was not in a good mood because I still had two bus rides ahead of me. Near the parking lot on Boulevard Rabatau, I heard a furious honking and looked around to see what was going on. The passengers of a DS were waving to me. I thought for a moment that I had dropped something—but no! My dear Carolina, I saw the tall silhouette of my first employer, the doctor, headed in my direction, chivalrous and smiling: "We really do see everyone at the Fair. Do you want to get in? The girls are with us: we'll make room and drop you at your nearest bus stop."

I didn't need to be asked twice, my legs were like cotton and my stomach was hollow because, after calling out to customers all day, I lost the desire to eat my sandwich at lunch.

The girls said to me: "B'jour!"

And the man struck up a conversation: he had plenty of time, given the crowd of cars inching along ahead of us up the boulevard.

He asked about my family and promised to return to the fair to buy some spices from me. He made a point of saying that he wanted to find a West Indian woman for his wife. For him, so chivalrous, what wouldn't we do? But for his wife? I'm not crazy!

Chapter Seventeen

September 20, 1963

Today, Carolina, my job was inhumane. I wasn't allowed to go to the bathroom, in case I missed a customer. I've already lost four kilos—I recommend hawking wares if you're trying to work on your figure. It's unbelievable how many people come to the fair! There are people who don't visit any stalls, they simply rush to the outdoor market to eat. I've watched so many people devour loads of sandwiches, another reason I've lost my appetite.

Just opposite my stall, a pied-noir had the smart idea to grill merguez and sell them spiced with harissa. Crowds rush to his stand from the other side of the Mediterranean: "Merguez grilled over a wood fire: come and get one!"

And they come, and the merguez really are grilled over a wood fire. The shack where I work with my boss is divided into four stalls filled with smoke all day long. By noon we can't tell what we're smelling, because the harsh odor of grease mixes into the lingering stench of the black smoke invading the space. Sometimes a cheeky mistral transports a perfumed cloud of Spigol spice mix to the opposite stall, while my boss rubs his hands together: "Oh! Look at the Italian wines over there! By the end of the fair, they'll be smoked like herrings!"

These reflections don't distract him for long, though, because he immediately adds: "Maméga! Pounce on the passersby! Pounce! They're eating instead of buying spices! Look, they're lining up at Landouillard's. He's going to put us out of business with his pâtés from Auvergne! Mesdames and messieurs! Some pepper for your pâté sandwich, it gives you strength!"

After this harangue, I'm at it again: "Buy some spices, mesdames and messieurs!"

A few frenzied eaters then approach and buy things as they watch me speak. The buyers are bizarre, one only wanted a tube of saffron, I would have given it to him gladly, but a merciless look from my employer makes me "pounce": "You don't need anything else? We have tea, the best kind! This powder: you can put it in any sauce, you can also drink it as an herbal tea, it's good for aches and pains."

I don't know anything about that, the boss said it to me, I repeat it, and now the eater leaves with several tubes of grayish powder that smells like rabbit fricassee!

The majority of people come out of curiosity: "Oh! A negress!" They are accustomed to our presence in Marseille, but they don't often see us making a sales pitch. They stop and approach, and I manage to get them to buy dried parsley or small bottles of bay leaves even though all around them, nature generously grows these fragrant Provençal leaves!

There are some who come out of sympathy. The West Indian rum seller, who however does not want any West Indian employees, lends me an empty crate so I can sit between two big waves of customers. There is the enormous Landouillard, who addresses me informally and offers me cider at every opportunity. He told me about all the places that hand out free samples; fortunately I am neither hungry nor thirsty, or else I'd leave each night with serious indigestion. And I also have an admirer, a refrigerator seller who adores ravioli. When my lover passes at noon with his plate of pasta in red coulis and approaches our stall to ask me when I'd like to go to a restaurant with him, my boss gets angry. He pinches his nose and yells: "Shoo! Shoo! You're keeping the customers away!"

He takes off, leaving me to detect a group of buyers who need no pitch. These are smart ladies armed with nets and shopping bags filled with household appliances, most often frying pans. They are meticulous and have prepared their shopping lists in advance. The boss recognizes them: these are the good mistresses of the house who fear neither diabetes nor cholesterol. They ask for vanilla for creams and ice creams, extracts for cakes, spices for the Christmas turkey.

With them, my boss is all smiles, his voice softens, there is no demonstration to perform, he takes their money, he's smooth. Once the customer who knows what she wants has walked away, he rubs his hands together and cries: "Maméga! That was a success!"

I know it was a success! And the person who scored it for him deserves a colorful paper hat and a bonus. I have to say as I hand them their purchases: "If you've forgotten something, don't hesitate to come back, I am at your service."

If I neglect to recite this phrase, watch out! But I pray to God that the shrewd housewife will not return, because then, for a few long minutes, I'll have to improvise a meal on the spot that incorporates the ingredients she bought.

There are also pretty people who look disdainfully at those eating the pâtés, salamis, and creams. They are svelte, and judging by their contorted faces, all those culinary aromas must tickle their nostrils and especially their stomachs! But the line, that damned line dissuades them from the merguez, they avert their gaze and pass by quickly. I enjoy calling to them: "So, madame, you're leaving without buying any spices? There's no good cooking without spices! Have you tried Chinese soup? We have shrimp and dried mushrooms."

Sometimes they give me an annoyed look, sometimes they answer kindly: "I'm on a diet, thank you."

People who are on a diet and walk over to the sampling area! Nonsense!

Finally, there are the people who remember. They head toward me, they don't look at the display on the counter but at my face as they approach:

"Hey! I was in Fort-de-France for three years! The coconuts weren't this expensive over there, were they?"

"I'm from Douala! Blackwater fever made me return, and now they have independence. I miss my houseboy!"

"Oh! A doudou! A doudou!* I had one during the war, I had one during the war, I was on the *Béarn,* I stayed in the West Indies for three years, I had a wife, how I loved her!"

"Diego-Suarez! The bay! The rougails, the ramatous!"†

Men, women, or children recall the too distant past with regret, nostalgia. It relaxes me and makes me forget the incessant music played morning and night on the fair speakers, I try to chat with them a bit; the boss appears and says: "Would these messieurs-dames like to buy something?"

* A term used in France for a Caribbean woman.—Tr.

† Rougail is a blend of ingredients including ginger, thyme, peppers, and tomatoes, used especially in Creole cuisine. A ramatou is a domestic worker, especially in Madagascar.—Tr.

They retreat, taking their enchanting memories with them.

What really makes my boss blow his top is when a colored person like us laughs at the civilized-looking vanilla arranged in glass tubes, and the cinnamon bark modeled, chiseled, cut symmetrically, waiting for buyers. The Africans grab the tube of ground kola nuts and say: "What is this? This isn't the real stuff! It looks like little pebbles."

I laugh to myself but even so I recite a speech on the necessity of packaging that reduces the kola nuts to lentils. Then comes a naive West Indian, he asks my boss: "How many chilis do you put in that jar for five francs! There's only enough for two fish soups! Come on, come on, you're kidding me! I'll have some sent to me from over there!"

Others maliciously eye the containers of breadfruit and ask me: "Did you divide a single breadfruit across all these containers?"

The boss turns green with rage: "Shoo! Blacks don't buy anything! They would rather order cases of hare pâté for Christmas! Do you know at least whether they're selling you cat?"

Sometimes I manage to calm him down: "You see, looking at your display, they picture, like me, gigantic breadfruit trees around their huts, and vanilla infused with musk perfuming the markets where they're from. These products are so pressed, so dried, how could they not want to smile? But it's not mean!"

I defended their cause again this afternoon when a blonde woman came by. She told me that she was West Indian and spoke to me in Creole: "A hurricane ravaged the islands, there's nothing left standing . . . People died, apparently . . ."

Emotional, I forgot my boss's instructions forbidding me

from responding to West Indians. The woman started to cry quietly, one by one her tears fell onto a row of barley sugar sticks in front of her. The boss, hardened by his own peace of mind, took out a feather duster to clean the already spotless tubes: "It's as though the hurricane blew through the merchandise! It's raining here!"

The béké shook my hand and took off.* The boss grumbled: "Luckily there are foreign countries to remind these women that they're just like everyone else!"

The news arrived from the surrounding rum stalls, circulated by the punch-drinkers. I found out that the hurricane that had ravaged the country was called Edith. The most unbelievable rumors ran wild, the big Landouillard said to me while chewing on his eternal cigarette butt: "If a hurricane could push Martinique to Vieux-Port, I wouldn't have to buy such expensive rum!"

It didn't matter how many times my boss said to me: "Pounce! Go on and pounce! You're letting the merguez seller scoop up all the customers!"

I couldn't do it anymore, Carolina. A mother's house sent flying, her house, her reason to live, along with that of everyone her age who will never move into subsidized housing, as luxurious as it is! And where were they at this moment, all those women without a place to live?

That thought was enough to give me a terrible migraine. Two hours before closing, I threw in the towel: "I'm going home! Can you deduct two hours from my pay?"

*The term béké refers to a descendant of white European slaveowners or colonizers/settlers in the French overseas territories, especially Martinique.—Tr.

I removed my madras and my collier-choux, which had been strangling me since I found out that Edith was gallivanting through the West Indies. I jumped in a taxi and arrived home just as my kids were coming back from school. They had heard too, a few of their classmates had told them about the hurricane. They knew all about the surroundings of Grandmother's hut, I hadn't spared them any details, and they were devastated: "What about the plum tree, do you think it fell? And the breadfruit tree, could the wind have . . . !"

I was the family haven, where each person gathered themselves and calmed their anxiety, but my husband and I couldn't relax, thinking about how back in our country, our people were perhaps searching at that very moment for a shield against the sun or a shelter for the night. It was horrific to feel so powerless in the face of such brutal adversity. We wanted to be with them and share their misfortune. When people laugh, they rarely need friends to think of them, but when they cry, how sweet it is for them to be understood and consoled!

September 29, 1963

Can you believe it? The big Landouillard came to give me clothing for the victims! I told him to go to the office in charge of gathering donations. He had piously collected coats, blankets, and woolen underwear in a suitcase. I couldn't tell him that after a hurricane, the sun casts its warm gleam over the misery left behind by its rival, the wind.

In the anthill where my people are collecting their scattered hopes, the inhabitants must be running, sweating, nailing, transporting beams and sheet metal. They must be lining up to receive bread, clearing the roads, they must also be arguing over buying a scrap of meat. All of this makes the tropics even hotter, but how can I explain this to Landouillard, so spontaneous in his charity?

October 1, 1963

The elites are organizing a special event for the victims. How can they exploit all these tears for a publicity stunt? How can they dance, have a roll in the hay, while the jazz punctuates the distress of those over there grinding their teeth?

A great cry rises from my people and I feel the pain deep within me. The vile thing refuses to leave its new home in the Caribbean sea; it spins around, demolishes huts in Cuba, in Guadeloupe, and from the Dominican Republic to Mexico the poor terrified people wait.

I received a few distressed words from my family and, powerless, I wiped away a tear while my husband read the letter in front of the counter. My boss became fatalistic, he said harshly: "You'll see how many negroes will soon come here instead of staying to rebuild their huts . . . And they'll never buy anything!"

Oh my God! How shameful, the people who think of nothing but how much money they can add to their full coffers! I wanted to run away, but I said to myself: "Four more days, and then it will be over."

October 3, 1963

Everyone is packing up at Parc Chanot, from the souks to the army pavilions, nothing left but the exhibitors who swarm the post office to send off their letters or register a change of address. The refrigerator seller asked me to go to Dijon for the next fair in November, I'll work for him and we'll eat ravioli. I bought a bottle of Italian wine and Pyrex glasses, just to bring something back from the fair. I know it's much more expensive than in the department stores, but oh well.

Blue screens, red screens lower, striped umbrellas, checkered umbrellas fold up, ugly stalls and pretty stalls empty out, eating customers and strolling customers pass, indifferent, through the mountains of boxes that now block the alleyways. The SNCF cars collect the packages being sent directly to other fairs. People call to one another, the stallholders agree to meet in the most remote towns of France or Europe. The mistral blows and our sweaters are back on. The fair is over, and soon it will be nothing but a memory for me, Parc Chanot, my Black boss, the conversations about the hurricane. The students from surrounding universities who came to sell crêpes or Spanish trinkets gather near the fountain to debrief their season: how were their employers, how much were they paid. Soon, they will be back at college and for them too the image of the fair will fade as soon as they've reached the lecture halls. At the merguez seller's, I became friends with an enthusiastic young girl who was reprimanded because she didn't have a loud enough voice to catch the attention of passersby. She came to say goodbye, her arms full of stationery: "I didn't have time to see anything at the fair, I just bought some school supplies! Classes start up again soon . . . Goodbye!"

I filled the crates with tubes, this work had to be done meticulously. The boss yelled: "Come back next year before the beginning of the fair if you want to chat . . . "

The student shrugged her shoulders, she set off for her destiny. I filled the crates and set off for mine, without regret, without bitterness. This is how life is, so why bother analyzing it?

October 8, 1963

Madame Roland took my place for twelve days. She washed everything but ironed nothing, all the cupboards are full of clothes awaiting my arrival, and with no break I must make up for the time lost at the fair, plug up the holes that appeared during my absence. I also discovered that one of my kids swapped his math lessons for cowboy books; when I rotated his mattress I found a dozen of them.

I wonder why I wear myself out so much just to earn a few francs that soon fly away. I paid Madame Roland, I bought an umbrella and a handbag, two pairs of shoes and some bits and bobs for the children, and then there was nothing left. I wonder whether instead I should simply wait each day, like the birds of the Gospel, for the seed that God brings.

My husband came home fuming, with a newspaper clipping that had made its way around his worksite. It said that officials had gone to visit the villages affected by the hurricane and had found the inhabitants joyous and carefree despite their misfortune. Where did I hear this saying? "Often the unfortunate laugh and sing for us while they're crying for themselves."

If only those officials knew what happens when their backs are turned: the people trade their yams for a bit of rice or cod. I picture the elderly nailing for the thousandth time the planks that a thousand winds have blown off, and those who no longer have the strength to strike the hammer try to find the békés from France, hoping that in their big planes they will have thought to bring nails to hold down the sheet metal of their huts. I also see that the myth of eternal happiness in the islands is still alive and well after the hurricane, just as it was before.

"Jeez!" my husband said. "My friends asked me what we were going to do with the collection money, since the people over there aren't in need."

Meanwhile, my kids emptied their piggy banks to donate to the victims, they gathered all their clothing that they no longer need. To indulge them, I made their donations into care packages that will be nothing but a drop of water in the ocean of my relatives' misery. And my husband griped again: "Why did they have to laugh in front of that journalist?"

I know why. They laughed out of gratitude and they waited, desperately, for nails, for sheet metal and crates of supplies that the Motherland is supposed to send them. They laughed because they wanted to hug them but didn't dare: people are so bizarre, you never know how things will be interpreted! Besides, my dear Carolina, a journalist shouldn't take notes after a cataclysm on the heels of an official procession, but, armed with a camera and a good ballpoint pen, he should cross hills and rivers and he would see that laughter is all that remains for the unfortunate. Above all, he should not say that he is a journalist, because they will hide their hunger and prepare their hut for his arrival . . . And so yes, they laughed . . .

Chapter Eighteen

November 11, 1963

Madame Roland said to me: "I scratch your back, you scratch mine. My lady is letting her daughter throw a party Sunday afternoon while she goes somewhere in the snow. I'm staying here, but she asked me to find someone to help. Can you come? I looked after your little ones; do me this favor."

I went out in the rain to meet Madame Roland. When I arrived at the large villa on the Corniche I was in a fairly bad mood.

She led me to the immense kitchen where she was in the midst of preparing little sandwiches on pain de mie. She pointed at two large grapefruits and told me to stick small skewers of olives and cheese inside.

I heard a laugh, I saw a young girl in pants and ballet flats talking to another girl dressed in a cream suit. They were standing in a gigantic living room, unlike anything I'd seen before, filled with exotic flowers that had been flown in specially, according to Madame Roland. When they noticed me, the two girls came to greet me, all smiles: "I'm glad you came," one said.

This was the mistress of the house for the afternoon. The boys arrived on foot or by moped, or more often by 2CV: in no time at all the area surrounding the villa was transformed into a parking lot; the young people happily climbed the few steps that brought them to the driveway, then funneled into the villa.

The young girl in pants took her role very seriously, she found seats for her guests, smiled at them. She had put me in charge of an improvised coat check. Madame Roland quickly called for me: “Maméga, let the kids deal with their coats themselves: they’re already clearing out this buffet!!!”

Indeed, on the two tables arranged in a corner of the living room, the petits fours were disappearing as a group of famished youths, likely on a diet for some time, were chowing down without a thought for the others. I stationed myself near the tables and watched the little gluttons with an expression that made them put down their food.

A tape with uninterrupted dance music invited them to dance. They played hard to get, they laid the groundwork, they chatted, they prowled around, glass in hand: a slow song persuaded them, they wrapped their arms around each other. It was nice, with no drama, it could have gone on like that for a long time, which would have pleased the young host’s mother. But after the bamba came the twist. Europe fled, South America set up shop, and generous Africa finally took over the frenzied tape. I had seen all of these dances performed in the streets of Cotonou at a religious festival, with sun and cactuses in the background. Here it was raining and the squalls in the gray gulf visible not far from here made the sad droplets fly through the air. The kids paid no attention to the lady’s Louis XV decor, they had their own in mind. Others clapped their hands and stamped their feet to the rhythm. Madame Roland came over and said to me: “What a band of savages!”

Good heavens, so this is how young Europeans blow off steam! The people on the news say it's good for them, that we should let them. But I started to get angry, because a boy who had hair down his neck plunged the living room into darkness. The young girl turned the lights back on three times, but the long-haired man turned them off again with a laugh and the group cheered. I called to Madame Roland and she said: "Either he stops, or the two of us will throw him out the window. He's skinny as a herring; with his short jacket, you can see he doesn't even have butt cheeks anymore for us to kick. We'll send him packing."

Madame Roland is nicely padded with her 80 kilos: she took off the madras she was wearing on her head and rolled it around her waist as though she were about to carry a bunch of bananas on her shoulders. She planted herself in front of the light switches; I followed her. The young girl said: "You see, Madame Roland, he's had too much to drink!"

Madame Roland replied: "Too bad for him, he can go quench his thirst outside if he touches this switch again."

The long-haired boy seemed to have spent much more time in nightclubs than in judo class. He looked at Madame Roland, who had taken off her high heels to steady herself, and shot me a contemptuous look, because I had armed myself, just in case, with a large black umbrella that had been dripping in a porcelain bucket, and I was staring at the maniac without breaking eye contact. The others were yelling enthusiastically and shouting to their friend: "Go on then!"

They were hoping for an amusing intermission that didn't come to pass. The long-haired boy, fuming and still contemptuous, retreated: "She had to go out and find some negresses to stop us from having fun!"

Madame Roland didn't budge from her place: "Talk as much as you want!" she murmured. "You're nothing but a little spoiled brat, you won't cause mayhem in the lady's house while she's away!"

They looked for other ways to amuse themselves. Since they couldn't have darkness, oh well, they would embrace under the numerous 220-volt light bulbs adorning the crystal chandeliers! My dear Carolina, they really went for it! The girls clung to the necks of the boys as though to life preservers and the slow song that brought them together went on and on. Madame Roland bustled around, clanged the empty glasses she gathered, groaned when she passed, stood near the switches if a boy got too close. She railed when she caught a brazen dance partner kissing his sweetheart. They were probably minors trying to look like grown-ups.

Madame Roland decided that we had to come up with a plan of attack to stop them from making love once and for all. She asked for my help. She began by closing the door that led to the cellar stairwell, she closed off the library, the bedrooms, the little lounge where an eager couple had already fled. She said: "I haven't dusted in here yet." And she opened the bay windows: a cool breeze rushed into the room and managed to sober up the young people. The mistress of the house understood her maid's thoughts. She diverted her gaze each time she felt our eyes on her and refused to flirt like the others. She possessed a basic modesty that inspired respect for her person and, by extension, for ours.

Madame Roland called to her: "Mademoiselle, you have to be wary of those kinds of guys, you never know what ideas they have in their heads. You have to send them home at nine o'clock as your mother ordered!"

The young girl went on the defensive:

"Those aren't 'guys,' they're my friends!"

"Well then!" said Madame Roland, "you can tell your friends: if I see them enter one of the rooms I made sure to close, I'll call the police! I mean, come on! Band of little scoundrels! You relish squandering your youth! When you're old enough for military service you'll already be nasty old people. And mademoiselle, if you're not happy about it, too bad! Look, just look!"

The young people didn't appreciate this. Couple by couple, they left, the mopeds revved on the Corniche and the cars started their engines, horses at full gallop. It was only 8:30, but the party was over, thanks to Madame Roland. I washed the glasses and put away the silverware; I was eager to leave. The young girl hid in a room with her friend and we heard them grumbling about the disadvantages of having an elderly Martiniquan woman inculcated with the old-fashioned principles of the islands.

I thought the hostess was upset, but she emerged from her hiding spot all smiles, almost relieved: "You were right, Madame Roland, to make them leave: they were drunk. They're better behaved when they haven't been drinking!"

Unfazed, Madame Roland replied: "Did you really need to have sparkling wine delivered, or take liqueurs from the cellar, when your mother suggested fruit juice? . . . Anyway, they'll hang themselves somewhere else, that's the important thing!"

The young girl wasn't used to hearing such language, her eyes widened in astonishment, she smoothed her short hair distractedly and kept smiling. Deep down, I thought, she must not be such a bad girl, but with a group like this, she won't stay that way for long.

It was still raining: I waited for a taxi outside, under an umbrella. I had to hurry because the next day, a Monday, I had to send my entire brood to school. I earned 5,000 francs for my extraordinary extra hours, and yet I am still asking myself, how much longer will my sisters have to look after girls who throw parties! Or wipe the little ones after they pee, or be on duty when all the world is dancing.

At Vieux-Port, despite the rain, the cafés and restaurants were full, La Canebière shined with all its lights and inspired hope. I stashed away my thoughts and returned home to tuck in my children who were waiting for me.

They don't know where I'm coming from, except for my husband. When I left this afternoon, I told them that I was going to visit a friend. Now they all wanted to know: Who was this friend? Where did she live? How was she?

I told them that she was pretty, that she served punch in fine crystal glasses and made her fruit juices in a silver tureen, but that she was very unhappy, because she didn't know anymore whether she was young or very old!

And so I put an end to tonight's whys and hows.

November 15, 1963

Our protégé came to say his goodbyes, he's leaving for an internship in Nantes . . . Nantes in November, he's in for an adventure! He will do masonry. His mother sent him his suitcase filled with lightweight suits, he's just bought his only wool sweater, and I am having a hard time getting him to take an old but comfortable and warm pair of pants for the construction site. He bought coveralls! For now he conflates Nantes with Marseille; since both cities are in France, how different could the weather be? He discovered that the mistral was not the gentle breeze that blows where we're from, but he has deemed it tolerable. He didn't want to buy boots either, he thinks they "look funny." He doesn't have sandals anymore but wears his thin-soled shoes. Anyway, he'll have to go see for himself to finally become a man.

November 20, 1963

Not a lady in sight. My husband has gone to the quays for some extra work: "A damn good job," he says, "we're paid well, we eat well, there's fruit galore, we see other negroes recount their misery, but I don't expect to stay with them, we only earn good money once per month, the rest of the time it's unemployment and the negroes wait in Harlem for the work to begin again in La Joliette! You know Lucien, the big bruiser who used to be a boxer, he scrapes the salt off the ships, he scrubs, paints, and cleans them! It's a nasty job, but well paid, negroes rush there to get those jobs. He's already started to cough up his lungs from spitting so much. If Robert hadn't pulled strings for me, they wouldn't have taken me on, and who knows how long they'll keep me. If you saw the procession of negroes who line up for a job and are turned away from the quays, you'd understand why Harlem never empties out . . . They're selling all the boats! La Joliette is nothing like it used to be. I remember before the Indochina debacle! There were always three or four ships to unload at the same time, the West Indians could always find a job, now I ask myself how all those people haunting the quays make a living."

I hear enough from the girls who are brought over, I can't worry about negroes searching for bananas on the quays! So, Carolina, I turned a deaf ear, but my husband continued: "I'm working at the quays for some extra money, we'll put it aside, you won't need to go to a 'lady' anymore, or pawn your typewriter at Christmas . . . It pains me when you leave for their houses, like our grandmothers, like our great-grandmothers, as if nothing has changed in all this time for us . . . Meanwhile they're making atomic bombs, talking about free peoples. I don't understand why you do it."

Well, I did it, and I will probably do it again. That's the way things are. I can't stop thinking about it: the West Indian women who come en masse to work for these ladies.

November 23, 1963

My dear Carolina, when vile things are afoot, it saddens my soul. The radio broadcast the atrocious news and I couldn't hold back my sobs: "My God, why have You allowed this to happen?"

The children wanted to know: "What's wrong, maman? Why are you saying that?" They surrounded me and they too were on the verge of tears just from seeing me cry, their little faces tense.

"They killed President Kennedy," I said.

"Why? Who is Kennedy? Is he the father of the little girl, poor thing?"

And the questions flew from every direction.

I answered: "He probably died so that Black people like all of you would be able to go to school without being harassed!"

The little ones didn't understand, they'll have plenty of time to learn, and whenever I can avoid disillusioned explanations, I do so. This didn't stop me from mourning the man who was taking a page out of Abraham Lincoln's book, he was only at the first chapter, and already the gust of wind has ripped off the branch, so green and full of hope. My potatoes are harder to peel than usual, and my tears won't dry up, because today their source is too significant. I cry because children don't have a father anymore. I think he died for men to be free. I cry because once again I was wronged. People no longer say: "My God! Protect those You sent to me as spiritual and mortal leaders." If the new generations still said that, they would understand that the institutions are permitted by God, that crime brings about nothing just or good. The person who commits regicide is a damned soul, even if the person he struck down is a bad man.

These thoughts hound my old mind that should be worrying about other things, housekeeper things: the price of polishing wax, the new scouring brush for automatic ovens, and other things will turn me into a robot. But there you have it, across the ocean, hundreds of thousands of Black men and women grope around in the night of their past and their present for a path that will lead them to lasting dignity; that's why, Carolina, I mourn the man who extended his hand to me. I cry and my Black face creases, my gray hands are antsy, and my heart is shaken along with the hope of mankind placed in a man. From Johannesburg to Mississippi, passing through Douala and Fort-de-France, people of color must be as emotional as I am. Blinding, a lightning bolt crisscrossed the black night of Black people, and I grieve as though for my father. I am ashamed for this century, so primitive that it shattered Kennedy's stubborn forehead. I couldn't speak to anyone, I decided that this would be a day of mourning. The children left to do the shopping, which allowed me to avoid the baker and the grocer, always eager to joke around.

Later this afternoon I received a visit from the little old lady, who's back from the nursing home: "I'm here! I thought of you when I found out that a young numbskull had killed Kennedy! They probably killed him to keep down the Blacks over there!"

The Blacks over there! What an egotistical and narrow-minded thing to say! I offered a cup of coffee to my old lady and retorted: "It's to keep me down, too! See my flattened nose! See my lower lip, it's to keep me down, too!"

She was surprised, my sweet Provençale. For her, so human, it wasn't an issue and I didn't want to insist on a matter that she had resolved with her heart. For a long time we chatted about everything and nothing and the afternoon ended without me realizing that my sadness had subsided. As we were listening to the news broadcast over the transistor, my friend said: "So the Occident and the Orient can only come together over a coffin, peace around a red wound . . ."

November 25, 1963

I finished my cleaning quickly and went to see my sweet old lady. When she spotted me, she cried out: "Here comes my Martiniquan!"

Finally, some progress: she didn't say "negress." I dusted all the rooms while she told me what she had done during her trip to Roque-d'Anthéron. She also spoke to me about Beaucaire, Sisteron, and Miramas, where she has grandchildren. And for the hundredth time, I described for her my mother's shack and the trees that surrounded it. What she doesn't understand at all is the winters that never come, and for her sake, I want to forget that other women with blue eyes have cold hearts.

Chapter Nineteen

December 5, 1963

Our protégé wrote to us: he's freezing and misses Pointe-à-Pitre.

"I can't feel my feet when I'm at the worksite, but I'm happy to be learning a trade. When my sister comes, she won't need to go straight to a lady's house—yes, West Indian women do that here in Nantes, too. I've come to realize that all of France is stocked with Martiniquan and Guadeloupean women, it embarrasses me . . . "

It worries me that he's embarrassed, because he'll rush to marry a mainland woman, and he will quickly forget Pointe-à-Pitre, his sister, and his present concerns.

December 10, 1963

I wrote to that literary agent, I told him that my letters will soon be finished. It's true, Carolina, there is nothing left to tell you that you don't already know. The days resemble each other, the years too, the ladies will always be the same, anonymous and sad. The human livestock brought over from my country will be distributed haphazardly through all the little villages of France. It will go unnoticed and soon simply be the way things are. The student with a sister working for a lady will avoid speaking about it, and the sister in the lady's home will deny it: and all will be well for the happiness of the few.

If my typewriter hasn't left for the pawnshop when these thoughts torment me, I will write other things so that I too can forget, and yet . . . There is Renée who came to tell me how, for an entire afternoon, she filled an enormous basin to water all around her employers' cabin, in need of gardening despite the winter. There is Madame Roland who will come to ask me for another helping hand. There is rue Paradis and Saint-Giniez where girls of color rush into the elevators of high-class buildings. There are all the ports of France that welcome those who land like bees on the dreadful flower of servitude. But I can't keep worrying about that, I need to mind my own business. So what should I do?

December 23, 1963

Solange is fully Parisian now, she goes to the theater when she can, dashes into the metro, adapts to the rain, and is in the know about everything. She wrote to me and now I have to make a choice about what she's cooking up:

"I wanted to sell my pavillon in Villejuif to buy a small apartment in Strasbourg Saint-Denis, but my husband didn't want to. And yet it was a good idea, I wouldn't have had to take the metro to work. I still think of the little restaurant that would make us a fortune. Are you still writing? I already told you that it's 'nonsense,' worse than sewing shirt collars for manufacturers. At least we make half a franc for those, whereas you can't eat words with vinaigrette or white sauce, so, my dear, let it go. Once I've found a place of interest, I'll tell you and you can think about moving, start talking to your husband about it now so he can get used to the idea of no longer hearing the wind blow over Vieux-Port . . .

"I went to a party where there were many negroes, they mentioned BUMIDOM, an office that, I think, was created to bring over negresses officially, so that the ladies will no longer need to 'bend over backwards' to pay for their trips, they'll just have to make a phone call and everything they need will be at their fingertips. There are people for it, I'm against it, what about you?

"I ate oysters."

December 24, 1963

Our protégé came to spend Christmas with us. It's very cold here, no one is taking a stroll through the mistral, so we invited him to spend the night with us. He didn't come alone: he arrived at the doorstep with another boy of color that we invited in because you don't leave someone outside in this weather, not even an animal. This friend told us that he was a student from the University of Caen. When it was time to sit down at the table, he wanted to leave! On a Christmas night, when there's enough food to feed eight people, there's enough for nine, unless the lady of the house is unwilling. But I was very willing, Carolina, because after his second punch, this boy initiated a long conversation in which I discovered that he was a nationalist. After the cheese, he spoke of the independence of all the West Indies and the confederation that they would form.

Then my husband said: "And your father? What does he think of this? He had you just after World War II, he lived through the West Indian uprising, their long trek from America to Cassino, he almost lost his life in Royan, all he wants is for you to live in peace.* Will the nation that you will have made with your sweat and blood be able to last long where it is, within firing range of the American warships? People see them cruising off the coast of Fort-de-France."

The boy passionately reiterated that he would make sure to guarantee the neutrality of his country.

My dear Carolina, we should never shatter someone else's dream. I said to the boy, and I meant it, that I'll be terrified if a confederation is formed, because half of the confederation will try to break down the other half. That's not why I'm terrified, we always end up coming to an understanding with our fellow man, but at what cost! I have a mortal fear, fear of colorful helmets speaking every language coming to teach my elderly mother how to behave! After all, I have no shame admitting it, I'm not afraid of dying, because the dead simply go to heaven or hell, but I'm afraid of what comes next if I'm still alive. Some of the larger countries will protect us, and some won't, and they will come to explain it right under the breadfruit tree that provides shade

*In June 1940, the day after the surrender of Marshal Pétain's government and the formation of the collaborationist government, several thousand West Indians joined the ranks of the Resistance, remaining active until 1943. These "dissidents," incorporated into the West Indian battalions of the Free French Forces, participated in the Provence landing and then took part in the Battle of Monte Cassino, and fought on the fronts of Royan and Alsace.—Ed.

for the hut that I left back in my country! And I won't be able to do anything about it but cry! . . .

The boy lightened up, his laugh reverberated through the room. I am so used to seeing my young compatriots who live in Europe talk of nothing but parties and money that I appreciated him. In any event, better a boy with a dream than someone who thinks about nothing. To take our mind off things, we started to sing Christmas carols from an old volume that I have piously kept over the years. Gentle singing, bringing us back to our roots, as though we were at a gathering in the countryside back home. The nationalist watched us with pity, disdain, then, gradually, he forgot the revolution he carries inside him and started to sing "Jésus Christ né jôdi, il est né, il est bien né mes enfants." He was a boy again, happy to be among his own.

I learned shortly after that our protégé was not complicating his life with too many theories, he was here, that was enough. He had come back to Marseille to see the young girl who hadn't turned her nose up at him when he wore only a pink shirt.

"Florette's parents are difficult! Her father is Greek and her mother Armenian. They're decent to me, but they're not thrilled. They never speak French when I'm there!"

A matter of the heart, I simply complimented him on his choice and wished him great happiness. The young boys took the first bus in the morning and returned to the city with their plans and their dreams.

I'm not ready to go to bed, I have so many things to write to Solange that I don't know where to start. A book perhaps! May God grant me the time to draft it, and protect those preparing to come and find their daily bread.

February 1, 1964

Carolina, things aren't going well, I was too tired from taking care of my five kids to resume that horrible profession of cleaning woman. Suddenly, I felt the weight of the years, prematurely, certainly, but I felt it. I have the illness of the century. I thought it was only the bons vivants bursting with money who were at risk of a heart attack, but my blood pressure has started to rise like I'm an elderly heiress. I realized it last week at the butcher's where I was working as an assistant. I was scratching the tables with a kind of scraper to get rid of the remnants stuck to the wood. I saw a thousand butterflies flying around my head, something like a black halo surrounded my eyes, and somehow I ended up sprawled on the ground. The panicked butcher called for help. Now I've returned to the fold, I don't want to go to the hospital. I'm still on the hunt for work so I can travel, earn money, and find an editor. My manuscript is finished, the word "fin" appears on the last page, and I am immobilized.

Easter 1964

Each day is different and each day is alike. Carolina, I won't tell you about all the medicine I'm taking to lower my blood pressure, that's another story. Despite all that, my hope is reborn, because people are reading my manuscript, they're talking about a review committee, Black writers have accepted my pages for review. People are reading me—Maméga! I know that they're all completely broke, but they're extending their hands to me, I forget about my pills, I jump for joy.

June 23, 1964

The laboratories, the tedious and endless tests of my entire anatomy: "We need to find the cause of your illness," the doctors say.

Be my guest! At the hospital the catheter works its way through my arteries, the urography is followed by other things with complicated names. Meanwhile, I feel an immense grief deep within me: Solange's body was crushed in the middle of a crosswalk on a major boulevard. She won't have a pied-à-terre in Strasbourg Saint-Denis. Her savings will go toward buying a nice coffin. She will also enjoy a permanent retirement in the land of her ancestors. A plane will bring her body back to our country. She must have had a few good jokes in mind that night, at least she's laughing on her way out. In her village's small cemetery, white sand and conch shells, pink and pearled, will adorn her grave.

It's hot and the shrubs shrivel under the glare of the scorching sun. My pages trundle along, they pass from reader to reader. Despite the lack of serious commitment, I feel that the day will come when my book will find a taker, and this helps me forget that for now I work as an assistant and have been transformed into a carpenter! I became a "nanny" to look after a blond angel, and they transformed me into a cook! What am I saying! I've been, I . . . I didn't have a choice, others chose for me, this is what goes through my head, without bitterness, it's hot, I can write under my favorite pine tree while the cicadas chant, Solange laughs next to me, what a prank she pulled on me, leaving like this! The others, Yolande, Renée, Madame Roland, will say in a few years to their children, to their relatives: "You're lucky! You're at the best schools! You're in the department stores and everywhere else you can gain access to by your merits, no one is amazed! In our day, all we could be was cleaning women! Things have really changed, believe me!"

Oh yes, Carolina! I believe it! I await this change!

FRANÇOISE EGA (1920–1976) was a writer and labor activist. Born in Martinique, she moved to France during World War II, where she met and married her husband. The couple lived in Djibouti and Madagascar before settling in Marseille, where four of her five children were born. Throughout her life, Ega was a prominent community leader and advocate for Caribbean migrants; in Marseille, she founded afterschool programs and tutored children, organized two labor associations, helped migrants with paperwork and transactions, and oversaw adult literacy lessons. In the 1960s, Ega composed two autobiographical works, *Le temps des madras* (1966) and *Lettres à une Noire* (*Notes to a Black Woman*), which was not published until after her death, in 1978; she also authored several novels. Since her death, her writings have been recognized as important works of twentieth-century postcolonial literature.

EMMA RAMADAN is an educator and literary translator from French. She has been awarded the PEN Translation Prize for Abdellah Taïa's *A Country for Dying,* the Albertine Prize for Anne F. Garréta's *Not One Day,* two NEA Fellowships, and a Fulbright. Her other translations include Maud Ventura's *My Husband,* Meryem Alaoui's *Straight from the Horse's Mouth,* and Abdellah Taïa's *Living in Your Light.*